PORTRAIT OF THE AUVERGNE

Portrait of

THE AUVERGNE

TRAVELS THROUGH A HAUNTED LAND

PETER GORHAM

ROBERT HALE · LONDON

© *Peter Gorham 1975*
First published in Great Britain 1975

ISBN 0 7091 5164 0

Robert Hale & Company
Clerkenwell House
Clerkenwell Green
London EC1 0HT

Composed by Specialised Offset Services Ltd, Liverpool
and printed in Great Britain by
Lowe & Brydone Ltd, Thetford

CONTENTS

ILLUSTRATIONS

Between pages 48 and 49

Puy de la Vache and Puy de Lassolas
Puy de Sancy
Château de Tournoël
Château de Chazeron
Notre Dame du Port, Clermont; tympan over south door
The Cathedral; Clermont
Royat; La Source Eugénie
Thiers; Maison du Pirou, sixteenth-century
Thiers; bridge over the Durolle
Thiers; Cutler at work
Medieval paper-making at the mill of Richard le Bas above Ambert
Ruined fortress of Mauzun
La Bourboule and la Chaîne du Sancy
Interior of Château d'Aultéribe

Between pages 96 and 97

Orcival; Romanesque church
Château de Cordes near Orcival
St Austremoine at Issoire – a storied capital
St Austremoine at Issoire, twelfth-century
St Yvoine from the Ribeyre
The Black Virgin of Vassivière borne through Besse

Auzon; Romanesque church porch
La Chaise-Dieu; Abbey church, fourteenth-century
Old Brioude from the Allier
Château de Chavagnac-Lafayette
Le Puy; Pic de St Michel d'Aiguilhe
Polignac, the château and the village
Lavoûte Polignac; castle on the Loire

ACKNOWLEDGEMENTS

The author would like to thank Monsieur Nicolas, archivist of *La Montagne*, and other members of the staff for much valuable assistance; Monsieur Pierre Rémy, of the same journal, who supplied the illustrations; and the staff of the University Library at Clermont, who were always kind and helpful.

TO G.S.

I

LANDSCAPE AND GEOGRAPHY

The Auvergne is a hard country: "The winds conflict, 'crossing' each other in continual dispute, the weather argues with itself", runs the saying. The region is also very beautiful and by no means dour on the whole; not so imposing as the Alps but, humanly speaking, more rewarding to the traveller, who may soon tire of the superhuman alpine grandeur; not so graciously inviting as Périgord or the Lot, perhaps, but geologically more varied, historically as interesting and certainly never so arid as the high *causses* of the Lozère and Tarn which fringe it to the south. It is not a country to travel in winter, at any rate off the main highways; for the minor roads which offer such delightful views, with infinitely varying perspectives of wooded valley, of bluffs surmounted by a ruined castle, of a village clutched into its hillside round a sturdy, dark-stone Romanesque church, are normally closed to traffic once the first snow has fallen. In high summer the climate is wayward. But where, in western Europe, is this not so? Spring, which carries over well into June in these parts, and the autumn — long, dry and hot even into late October — are the best seasons for the casual visitor.

The hardness, in fact, could now more precisely be described as remoteness, a quality these package-travelling, coach-encumbered times increasingly rare and much sought after by those who, while appreciating sun, good food and pleasant company, do not wish to sprawl like human kippers in serried rows along a beach they can hardly see for other heat-dried bodies.

This book is not intended as a factual guide (*Michelin Guide Vert* will give you all the statistical detail) but as an interpretation; a traveller's eye view of what is to be seen and how to get to it, a historian's insight into the human events which have helped to form the landscape. For one cannot know a people or a landscape without understanding how they have become what they are. By way of personal recommendation, the book should speak for itself. I can only add that, sceptical at first, I became enchanted as I went. I did not spend a year in the Auvergne in order to write a book but in the end could not help doing so. The whole region gripped me with its strangeness; its abrupt changes of climatic mood, architecture and landscape; its reticence, mirrored in the sharp, ironic temper of the people. And, later, I came to appreciate their friendliness which offsets that cool suspicion of the stranger, common to all mountain folk. In this part of France I have never asked anyone for help and not received it.

There is only one large city in the region: Clermont-Ferrand, to which I shall devote a short, separate chapter since its historical background and recent marked development are vital to an understanding of the region as a whole. As industrial cities go, Clermont is an amiable place but anonymous, like most contemporary administrative capitals. The smaller towns are cheaper and more convenient from the holiday-maker's point of view, for their quota of modest family hotels grows every year, and places like Issoire, Brioude and Aurillac have excellent shopping facilities. Soon, every large village will have not one but several hotels; most of them already boast an establishment rating one or two 'stars', awarded by an assiduous and systematic Regional Tourist Authority which bases its evaluation on national standards. Food is simple but good, in or out of high season. In twelve months, and in the course of several subsequent visits, I scarcely ate a bad meal and rarely paid more than I should have done for the pleasure. It helps a great deal to speak the language (as always in France), but a smile and the attempt to communicate in French works wonders. The Auvergnats are singularly honest in that they do not pretend to offer you more than they can, in fact, provide. They are also very practical people who are prepared to cater for children.

To conclude this short introduction it may be useful to summarise the geography of the region while leaving detailed description of each sharply defined area to its appropriate chapter. The principal and unique feature of the Auvergne is its volcanic hills which form, as it were, the geological vertebrae of the Massif Central, rising abruptly from the gently folded plateau of the country to the north, known as the Bourbonnais because it was the original home of the Bourbon family who, in the person of Henri IV, succeeded to the throne of France in the late sixteenth century. Most travellers will come this way, down the main Paris-Clermont road or via Bourges — to the north-west — ancient capital of the Berry, a rich agricultural region known for the excellence of its cuisine. The latter route, which takes you through Montluçon, dominated by what remains of a fifteenth-century Bourbon castle, strikes across the valley of the Sioule, a pretty, sinuous river famous for its trout. It is a rather tortuous road, dropping steeply from time to time, only to climb again through a series of *enlacements*, to offer fine views across the rolling hills of Combrailles on either side. The other road, via St Pourçain and Gannat, is straighter and more direct but carries a heavier volume of traffic. These two routes meet just outside Riom. From here there is a double carriage-way into Montferrand, the industrial half of the twin city of Clermont-Ferrand.

Soon after Gannat the formidable 'Chain of Volcanoes' comes into view. On a stormy summer day blue-black and wreathed in swirling eddies of whitish-grey cloud, these peaks announce one aspect of the regional character — harshly forbidding at a distance but, on closer inspection, richly wooded in their hollows where the volcanic alluvium has weathered and settled. The Monts des Dômes are young as mountains go for they were thrown up about a million years ago, when Man first stalked ungainly upon this earth. These followed the period of cooling-off while glaciers carried down their laval matter eventually to form the rich soil of the *limagnes*, as the narrow plains are called here, through which the Allier, with its tributaries, runs like a broad gutter. Or, more precisely, like a central gutter serving two houses; for, to the south-east of the central *limagne*, rises another less sharply folded range of hills, the Monts du Livradois and, still further east on the far bank of the swiftly running Dore, a much higher range, the Monts du Forez. From the highest peak of the Forez, called Pièrre-sur-Haute, one can see on a clear winter morning — beyond the valley of the Upper Loire and the intervening hills of the Lyonnais — the first peaks of the Alps, some 150 miles away as the crow flies.

These two ranges are roughly parallel running north and south. The Monts des Dômes, whose splendidly arrogant cones are the dominating perspective from the roads leading into Clermont from north and west, march proudly south to join another range of mountains, even more violently rift and faulted, known as 'Les Monts Dore'. Their central peak, the Puy de Sancy, at 6,000 feet, is the highest in the Massif Central. Its chief rivals, the Puy de Dôme — towering over Royat, the principal suburb of Clermont — and the Plomb du Cantal, sometimes called 'the belly-button of France', are only slightly lower.

The landscape, however, changes markedly as one moves south. Most of the high country near Clermont has been made into a national park whose chief wealth is its timber; while the valleys on either side of the Issoire road are known for their vineyards (quite a lot of wine is produced but little exported) and orchards. Further south the high, bare plateaux of the Artense and the Cézallier, littered with morainic rubble poking up through the crisp, springy grass its watery soil nourishes all summer, give way to the beautiful valleys of the Cantal which run south-west between a rib-cage of steep-sided escarpments down to Aurillac, the commercial centre of this region. The Cantal is essentially cattle-grazing country, among the richest in France because the underlying rock is not porous and so retains its moisture throughout the hottest of summers. This is why the fields, even on the open plateaux, are always so green and trees so tall and abundant.

In times past, cattle were driven up from the plains of Languedoc to summer here and fatten on the rich grass. The lowland farmers repaid the graziers in terms of the fertiliser the cattle left behind them while the upland farmers also profited from the cheeses made on the spot from the cows' milk, storing them in caves, or in valley barns, to ripen during the following winter. Cheese-making is still a notable industry in the Cantal and in the Livradois. I can vouch for the goodness of its products, which are various and intriguing to the palate. The best known are the firm, saffron-coloured Cantal and the two blue-veined varieties, Bleu d'Auvergne and Fourme d'Ambert.

Below Aurillac, where the plain is a mere bowl into which flow the waters of the Jordanne and the Cère, lies the roughly triangular area of rounded hills and meandering valleys known as the *Châtaignerie* because of the wealth of its chestnut woods. This remote and charmingly unselfconscious countryside rises sharply to the south and falls even more abruptly to the gorge of the Lot, whose course here forms the southern boundary of the Cantal.

Strikingly different again is the high plateau south and east of the Plomb du Cantal. One hundred and fifty years ago, denuded of trees and scarcely cultivable with the scanty resources at the disposal of the local farmers, this upland must have been something of a wilderness in spite of the innumerable rivulets and streams that criss-cross its windy acres. Now, as well as good grazing land, it affords some arable farming. St Flour, the regional capital, is an interesting and prosperous city and an admirable centre for exploring this whole region rich in castles and splendid views. Especially is this so above the gorges of the Truyère whose wildness has not been spoiled by an elaborate system of dams and barrages similar to that on the upper Dordogne, on the western border of the Cantal.

The lower gorges of the Truyère are in the *Département* of the Aveyron but the country of the Margeride, pine-forested in the north, wild and sparsely populated everywhere, is legitimately part of the Auvergne. This remote region, whose geographical frontier is the upper gorges of the Allier, was the refuge of the *Résistance* of the Massif Central, and a great battle of which more will be said was fought out here in 1944. Beyond the gorges of the Allier, steeply folded country of considerable beauty, lies the Velay; its capital is Le Puy, of the strange conical crags that travellers passing through to Provence and the Côte d'Azur so often wonder at but rarely pause to investigate. Administratively speaking the Velay is part of the Haute-Loire department: historically it belongs as much to the Auvergne as the Forez, whose lonely, silent pine-woods merge into it, so I make no excuse for including it in this book.

We have, indeed, now come full circle. The only area I have not mentioned is the undulating hill-country of Combrailles — neither so grand nor so variable, weatherwise, as the volcanic mountains of the centre. It is characterized by reedy, shallow lakes, lichened birch and beech woods, and attractive small towns like Auzances, Giat, Montel-de-Gelat and Bourg-Lastic, the latter ideal for exploring the forested wildnesses of the gorges of the Avèze (a river which has given its name to a liqueur distilled from gentians) and those of the upper Dordogne.

What this whole region offers is tranquillity and the sense of wide spaces in which to enjoy it. Apart from the tyre factories of Clermont, fostered for seventy years by Michelin into a major source of employment, there is no heavy industry at all so that one may drive — quite literally — all day without seeing an industrial chimney or, indeed, anything more visually offensive than a stone-quarry; and there is as yet, the eastern approach to Clermont excepted, no suburban sprawl. The only ugly town I know is Bort-les-Orgues, and the ugliness here is confined to a small sore of industrial housing on the outskirts, barely visible from the main road and deriving from the construction of the great dam just above the town. Nor is there any pollution worth speaking of in spite of the somewhat casual French attitude towards the disposal of sewage. In the mountains I have often drunk from the streams and had absolutely no qualms about doing so.

Finally, this sense of quiet contributes to the 'haunted' quality of the high country. Stop the car and the silence is striking. After a while it imposes on the spirit; one grows into the quietness and nerves relax as the eye moves restfully from whispering stream to over-hanging wood and up to the blue vault of sky across which buzzard or kite trace their patient circles.

II

THE NORTHERN APPROACHES

Let us begin with two castles and two women. Leaving aside, for the moment, Clermont-Ferrand and its somewhat schizophrenic history, the traveller will find a number of interesting places within a twenty-kilometre radius of the city. One of the good things about Clermont is that one can so easily get out of it into a scenically varied and attractive countryside; for the outlying suburbs, a cluster of self-contained villages more rural than urban in their topography, are an integral part of the foothills of the Puy de Dôme.

The long, straight rue Blatin, leading into the Avenue Royat, passes through Chamalières, a fashionable quarter whose rentières depend heavily on *les curistes*, the ailing or retired who come year after year to drink the medicinal waters of Royat. Turning sharp right for Durtol, one climbs steeply past handsome modern villas to reach this high point from which there are splendid views back over the city, closely knit about the twin hillocks where the feudal *enceintes* of Clermont and Montferrand once glared at each other in suspicious rivalry. The inevitable and anonymous tower blocks are beginning to people the skyline here as everywhere else in western Europe; but the salient feature is still the twin-spired mass, in black Volvic stone, of the early Gothic cathedral: more than a trifle sinister it always seems to me — like a hump-backed ogre with two heads, each crowned by a tall conical hat.

From Durtol, in the direction of Volvic, a pleasant, gently winding road has been cut along the flank of the Puy de la Coquille. The sub-tropical luxuriance of the vegetation is striking; no doubt the rich sedimentary soil accounts for this, and all kinds of shrub and fern flourish beneath the beech and chestnut trees. Yet the piles of grit left at strategic points by the roadside against the snow and ice of the winter are usually of pumice; and one does not have to climb very far above the tree-line before the soil becomes thin and the morainic outcrops begin to poke through the grass. To the right the orchards of Blanzat and Nohanent, in spring delicately pink and white against the lush green of these hillsides, look across the Grande Limagne, some twenty-five miles wide between Riom and the river Dore, close by Chateldon. If you are in the mood for dawdling (and it nearly always pays to dawdle in the Auvergne, which is not, as I shall hope to make clear, a region for precise itineraries) there is a natural belvedere just above the turn to Argnat from which Thiers, nestled about the first spur of the range known as *Les Bois Noirs,* is visible in fine weather.

From here the road descends to Volvic, whose quarries furnish the black volcanic stone of which so many of the villages of the 'Chaîne des Volcans' are built. The town has a dignified church off its central square, one of the few good modern rebuildings in the Romanesque style. Though tastefully picked out in white, in high contrast to the light-absorbing mat texture of the local stone, the interior is not remarkable as interiors go in this region so rich in sculptured capitals. But it has a pleasing 'Virgin and Child' modelled on the famous one, 'Our Lady of the Marthuret', at Riom. The church is dedicated to St Priest, a seventh-century bishop martyred in this town, whose oddly Anglo-Saxon name recurs frequently all over the Auvergne: it is connected, too, with St Avit, a great builder of churches who brought here, from Issoire, the remains of St Austremoine, the very first christian bishop and martyr of the region and its patron saint. The region's early history is littered with martyred saints, and these three (together with St Genès, an actor who satirised Christian rituals only to reveal inadvertently, in the presence of a Roman governor, that he was a Christian himself) are the most commonly remembered.

Volvic owes its past renown and present prosperity to its situation on the *cheire* or runway of lava which flowed down from the Puy de la Nugère, the most northerly of the chain of peaks stretching from here to Besse-en-Chandesse. So hard is this grainy lava that it could not be cut until the fine-tempered steel tools of the thirteenth century became available: which is why most of the earlier churches were built of the lighter-coloured, more attractive stone known as arkhose. The quality of volvic is so hard it can be subjected to extremely high temperatures without flaking. It is widely used by the chemical industries and, being virtually impermeable, by Michelin for their road signs all over France.

After the sombre enclosed atmosphere of Volvic, the story of the spirited lady of Tournoël, the castle close by, is marvellously gay and extrovert if a shade naughty. Leaving the town as if for Riom you must climb to the castle by a steep, narrow lane winding off to the left from the main road. Suddenly, the enormous craggy pile hoves into view as one enters the hamlet of Tournoël, a favourite Clermontois rendez-vous for those Sunday lunches that linger satisfyingly into the afternoon. At first sight the castle looks almost intact; only on entering the courtyard, after rounding the western walls, does one realise it is merely a shell although some parts of the interior are quite well preserved. Once it had four curtain walls but these have been heavily pillaged by local builders during the past 200 years: a not uncommon occurrence after the Revolution, when such places were looked upon as untimely reminders of the feudal past. The interior contains some handsome vaulted passage-ways and emblazoned portals of the fifteenth and sixteenth centuries; while the huge donjon tower — its sheer potence still astonishes, patched and mended though it is — offers magnificent views across the countryside to east and south. Yet it is the story of Dame Françoise de Talaru that endears Tournoël to the visitor.

Originally a typical medieval fortress, the castle was rebuilt in the more civilised and less turbulent years of the mid-fifteenth century by Jean de la Roche, a great-grandson of a High Chancellor of France, who had married a wealthy heiress of the Sorel family. It was their son, already well into middle age, who took to wife the young Françoise de Talaru, only to leave her a widow at 21 with a young daughter, Charlotte, to bring up. Now the fate of heiresses in these times was always precarious but the situation of an heiress without a father and protected only by an inexperienced and nubile mother was apt to bring out the worst in her neighbours, even if they happened to be relatives. At any rate, Dame Françoise had little choice but to place her child in the tutelage of an uncle, a canon of Cébezat, a monastery on the plain near Clermont. The latter promptly and shamelessly began to pilfer certain revenues of his ward. Françoise therefore banished him from the castle and took Charlotte into her own personal care. The priest, however, was not so lightly dismissed. In the crafty way of his kind, he denounced her for immoral behaviour as a "Mélusine, Circe, witch and sorceress" to the senior magistrate of Montferrand, one Albon St André (whose arms may be seen on the fine chimney piece of the room adjoining that of the Chatelaine). In 1501 — after some deliberation that surely did not preclude his considering the case as a means to purely personal ends — he declared for the canon, to whom he gave back the wardship of the child. Furthermore, he ordered the Dame de la Roche to expel from Tournoël "that great collection of men-at-arms, hangers-on and other people unknown" which formed her entourage — reasonable enough on the face of it since a young widow was unlikely to be able to control such a gang. But one does wonder whether she would not have been completely unprotected without them. The point may have occurred to Françoise, who took the bold and unexpected way out of seducing the magistrate himself, perhaps on the principle of — if you can't beat them, marry them.

Anyway, marry the bailli St André she did and took the additional precaution of betrothing Charlotte to his only son by a previous marriage. St André doubtless thought himself well served. Unhappily for him he died three weeks after the marriage, leaving the nimble-witted Françoise still mistress of the castle, secure in her protection of the child, and pregnant. The envoi is less happy: her son, Jean St André, although a distinguished soldier and a Marshal of France, took to politics, allied himself with the arch-Catholic Guise family in the course of the Wars of Religion which so devastated these parts, and was eventually assassinated — by a Catholic.

The castle itself also suffered badly in the Wars of Religion. Battered in a siege by the Catholic League in 1594, it was retaken by the army of Henry IV the following year. In the seventeenth century it was neglected and crumbled in the fierce storms that whips these hills most winters, eventually to be bought, in 1766, by Guillaume de Chabrol, of the family that owns the beautiful mansion of Jozerand in the hills to the north of Tournoël. He was a Councillor of State and one of the first authorities on the folklore of the Auvergne. Tournoël remains in the possession of this family which, oddly enough, remembering the background to Françoise's story, is well known for its distinguished lawyers and soldiers.

The other tale concerns the castle at Châteaugay: it is not happy or amusingly scabrous and its outcome is wicked. Less hemmed-in by the hills that Tounoël, Châteaugay, some five miles due north of Clermont, sits handsomely enough above the gently sloping vineyards exposed to the morning sun that produce the best-known red wine of the region.

Like Tournoël, the castle's eminence dates from the fourteenth century, when it was built by the first Pierre de Giat, a Chancellor of France. It is his grand-son, another Pierre, who is the villain of the piece, whichever of the two tales relating to the murder of his wife, Jeanne, you choose to believe. The simpler of the two has it that he poisoned her: the other reads like the scenario for one of those dark-natured Renaissance melodramas written by our own Jacobean poets; for it shows the terrible fate of a woman, less adroit and more vulnerable than Françoise de la Roche, who allowed her beauty to be used for murderous ends.

At the beginning of the fifteenth century when France was less a kingdom than a number of feudal domains, quite divided against itself and scarcely able to recover from the dreadful defeat inflicted upon its chivalry at Agincourt, Pierre II of Giat was influential at the court of Charles VII (the Daupin of Shaw's *St Joan*). Court chamberlain and confidant of the King, and an inveterate intriguer, he made some enemies as ruthless as himself. He had married one of the beauties of the time, Jeanne de Noilhac, from the rich plains of the Berry. Now Jeanne, who was noted for her ability as a horsewoman — it is said her greatest pleasure was to hunt — was beguiled from such country pursuits to the corrupt court of Isabeau of Bavaria, queen to Charles VII. In the course of a sinister and complicated intrigue directed ultimately against the Duke of Burgundy, Jean Sans Peur, Giat first embroiled her with his greatest enemy, de la Tremouille; the latter then used her as bait to attract the attentions of the Duke, whose courage, wealth and ability (as well as his friendship towards the English) had made him the object of envy and hatred at the French court. Jeanne, it seems, was intended to be, if she did not actually become, the mistress of the Burgundian. Certainly she was used to lure him to

Montereau, near Paris, where he was assissinated at the connivance of Tremouille. Horrified, Jeanne returned to Châteaugay and her horse-riding, while her husband pursued his turbulent life at the Court.

Yet her fate was still dark, for Pierre took as his mistress another rich and beautiful woman, Catherine de l'Isle Bouchard whose morals, as it turned out, were as loose as his own. Whether the fast-living Pierre wished to marry the widow, or whether it had dawned on him that Jeanne knew too much of his intrigues for his own well-being, he ordered a servant to get rid of her. She was tied to the tail of one of her own horses, dragged to death over the rough ground and brought to the edge of a precipice at the edge of the estate, known as the 'Saut du Loup'. There, says the chronicler, "maddened by the last dig of the spur the horse dragging Jeanne's bloody body was driven over the edge . . . taking with it the remains of a woman who had been the wife of the High Chancellor of France". Then, cryptically: "After the death of his wife Pierre took as his second wife his mistress, Catherine de L'Isle Bouchard".

Destiny, however, had something in store for Pierre II de Giat. Not long after he had become Catherine's third husband he was lured to a castle in the Berry, strangled, sewn into a sack and dumped into the river. De la Tremouille is thought to have had a hand in this affair, too. We do know that he became Catherine de l'Isle Bouchard's fourth husband. This story, frightful as it is, seems too well documented, and too apt for the times and the people involved, not to be true.

The castle at Châteaugay passed from the Giat family to that of Laqueuille, who kept it until the Revolution when, as the property of emigrés, it was declared confiscated to the State and renamed Bel-Air. Fine air it certainly does have, as poor Jeanne de Noilhac doubtless appreciated. Some of the rooms in the donjon are in good repair. But, like most fine houses that have not been lived in for some while or carefully preserved in their original state, it has a melancholy atmosphere. People it with the characters of the story and one tends to feel it haunted. The room that was formerly the banqueting hall is called 'The Hell of the Gay Heart'. Was it purely imagination that made me turn round as if a troubled ghost had touched me on the shoulder?

Châtel-Guyon, though named after one of the grand and

haughty barons who so troubled the kings of France in the Middle Ages, has no ghosts unless it be those of departed Auvergne waiters lured to the siren Côte d'Azur in winter time and tempted to remain there by *la douceur de la vie*. For Châtel-Guyon is one of several spas that attract visitors from all over France to the Auvergne, between May and September. By mid-September, in fact, this charming little town, so oddly redolent of the gentler times of the Second Empire, is already half deserted. Return in October and most of the hotels are shut: the waiters, waitresses and chambermaids have indeed gone back to Menton or Nice to find work; or perhaps to 'rest' if the season has been good and the tips generous.

Henri Pourrat, easily the most readable and amusing of the several native historians of the Auvergne, catches the atmosphere of Châtel-Guyon very well. After noting the extraordinary number of sweetshops and the dignified reserve of the *pharmacies de luxe* staffed by serious young ladies and discreetly knowledgeable men in immaculate white coats, he goes on:

> How can one fail to smile at these grassy lawns, all vermillion and poppy red with flowers, these trim summer villas that reconcile the Norman style so attractive to holiday-makers with the Romanesque imposed on them by local pride. They have even contrived a roof-top for the bell tower, ornamental mouldings for the roof — and supports for the mouldings. Here one can understand better than elsewhere that life might even be supportable without its sensual pleasures.

An air of relaxed well-being does, indeed, pervade the place: the buildings are all white or cream or fawn, their detail picked out in pastel shades of blue and green — even boudoir pink. And the gardens, pace Monsieur Pourrat's sly verbal smile, are quite delightful, the borders a riot of colour, the small *pavillon*-style shops, their windows dressed with discreet elegance as if to encourage in the heart of some *curiste* who feels himself growing stronger every day on the medicinal waters, the casual dalliance of an impermanent *amour*.

Appropriately enough Maupassant took Châtel-Guyon as the model for his little town in *Mont Oriol*, calling it Enval — the name of a pretty village, famous for its chestnut trees, off the road to Volvic. Pourrat tells us that the writer suddenly felt the urge never to leave the place, but I am sure Maupassant would not have endured the winter there with the shutters up, the nasal, vivacious Menton accents gone, and no pretty, slightly-faded *dames d'un certain age* to eye hopefully in the comfortable, plush cafés.

There are some charming walks along the chestnut-shaded valleys to the west of the town and one of them will bring the traveller, in half-an-hour or so, within sight of the sombre brown walls of Chazeron, once the refuge of another Guy, a robber-baron so aggressive he brought down upon himself the anger of Philippe-Auguste. This king of France, whom the school books tell us invaded England in King John's time, routed Guy out of the place and distributed his lands among the lords of the royal army. As an afterthought he then annexed the whole province to his northern kingdom - the first time the Auvergne became officially part of France. Chazeron can only be visited on certain days and I was unlucky in choosing the wrong one. An imposing building (the best view is from the main road to Loubeyrat) it is basically medieval and was rebuilt in the seventeenth century. One of the last aristocratic owners, the Duchess Marie-Pauline de Brancas, was surprised to find herself, one day in 1791, literally sealed within her castle by a *commissaire* from Riom. Indignant, she presented herself before the Revolutionary council to be informed that she was listed as a royalist 'emigrant', a non-person who did not officially exist; on pointing out the error she was given a certificate of residence, and the bureaucracy then removed the seals of state. Legend has it there was, in fact, a banished *personnage* secretly in residence and that the village people were aware of this. The feudal heritage died hard in some parts of the Auvergne in spite of the poverty and the landlessness of its people.

The commissaire may have entertained some such thought as he rode back down the valley-road to Riom. This rather sober, withdrawn little town famous for lawyers and for a stubborn contest with Clermont, in Renaissance and later times, over its claim to be the administrative capital of the Basse-Auvergne, is worth a morning's walk.

Redesigned on a grid-plain in the late fifteenth century, Riom is architecturally quite the most homogeneous town of any size in the Basse-Auvergne. One's first impression that there is something missing is correct: the ring-road which now delivers the place from through traffic was formerly the site of the city walls. Within the precinct lies all there is to see. Riom often reminded me of certain Scots Lowland towns, proud of their historical past and not unduly concerned to reveal themselves to a stranger. Of its patron saint, St Amable, a curious story is told by Louisa St Costello, an English mid-Victorian traveller who has some tart comments to make on the unhygienic state of France at that time. After noting that he carried a perennial ray of sunshine in his glove "which obeyed him like a faithful servant", she observes that he disliked bad smells intensely: "One day a woman came to pray at his tomb; but, carrying a lamp filled with malodorous oil, she fell dead on the spot — struck down by St Amable, who was offended by the disagreeable smell". Miss Costello then adds with crisp Victorian disdain: "It is scarcely possible to conceive how he could have borne the Auvergne now". (I hasten to add that Riom is extremely clean and well kept).

The Romanesque portal of the church dedicated to St Amable first strikes the eye as one enters the old town from the Place de la Fédération; but the typically Romanesque apse, with its radiating chapels, is rather spoilt by the buttresses supporting it while the church lost its most imposing feature, an exceptionally high spire, in an earthquake. The interior is handsome but rather gloomy: if the sacristan can be found he will show you a beautiful reliquary in the form of a cross. And if you happen to be hereabouts in June, men in the traditional white dress of the Riomois carry the 'châsse' containing the saint's remains in traditional procession through the streets.

Most interesting to the casual visitor will be the façades and courtyards of the stone-built fifteenth-, sixteenth- and seventeenth-century houses in the main streets. Before searching out these, however, he will notice the very handsome clock-tower at the corner of the rue de l'Horloge and the rue St Amable, only slightly damaged in a preliminary bombardment of the town by the Germans in 1940. The curly 'flamboyant' window-heads and the fleur-de-lys decoration of the tower walls are delightfully neat and soberly elegant, in a style typical of Riom as a whole. Equally attractive are the wooden sculptures of the 'Maison de Bois' on the opposite side of the main street;

while a little further down is the handsome 'Maison des Consuls'— again reminding one of Scots 'baronial' with a perky, blue-filed turret on the corner. The most beguiling courtyard is that of the Hotel Guimoneau at No 12 in the rue de l'Horloge. Push open the door and go down the passage and you will be pleasantly surprised by a gracious stairway adjoining a Renaissance gallery with 'flamboyant' arches. The medallioned heads on the stone balustrades of the stairway are really fine: probably portraits of local folk, but classical in style, they look down with an elegant refinement of pose as if disdainful of this mundane twentieth-century world.

Riom is essentially a place to wander through and its museums are well laid out and quite interesting: the pictures in the charming Musée Mandel are far better than those in Clermont which, it is fair to warn the artistically hopeful traveller, can only be described as execrable. One more building is certainly worth looking at: the Sainte-Chapelle whose façade abuts upon the garden at the end of the long main street. This chapel was built as an integral part of the huge palace erected by Jean, Duc de Berry, in the late fourteenth century. Of this grand but ineffectual character whom a modern historian has described as one of the greatest disasters ever to happen to the Auvergne, more anon. Of his palace nothing remains and the Sainte-Chapelle, his only surviving monument, now forms part of the huge Palais de Justice. Here the rapacious Duke was married, at the age of 49, to a girl of 12. One can imagine her looking up bewildered, and probably frightened, at the splendour of the chapel windows, paid for out of the sweat and toil of the beleaguered country-people and by a loan from the rascally Baron de Giat who had his wife murdered at Châteaugay. There were no children by this impurely dynastic marriage which united the Comté d'Auvergne to the Duchy created out of the Basse-Auvergne and the Bourbonnais to compensate Jean for the loss of his other domains to the English.

Finally, there is the Gothic church of the Marthuret, elegant and well proportioned, off the quiet southern quarter. It is renowned for the statue of the Virgin and Child, known as 'Notre Dame du Marthuret', which I do not find so moving as the best of the Virgins in many of the small churches. A gracious piece of work that narrowly avoids the sentimental.

Riom came briefly into the news in 1940 and 1941 as the scene of the famous 'trial' at which leading French politicians of the Appeasement era were put in the dock by the Pétainist regime, at the instigation of the German invaders. Daladier, Reynaud and Léon Blum, together with General Gamelin, were all confined at Chazeron throughout a winter of deep snow, the old castle ringed by German outposts and armoured vehicles against any attempt to set them free. Then, as the embattled world awaited some new barbarism, the trial was quietly abandoned and the politicians, separated, transferred elsewhere. A slightly sour envoi to Riom's long history of legal dispute.

Three churches in the vicinity of Riom are well worth visiting: the most famous, to which Pépin the Short, conqueror of the invading Moors, carried the remains of St Austremoine on his own shoulders, is also the most dishevelled. Mozac, now almost a suburb of Riom, grew up round the abbey founded there in the seventh century by St Calmin (who also built the great abbey church at Le Monastier, in the Velay, which we shall visit). Gybal, a fiercely patriotic local art-historian, rightly describes Mozac as "*une église assassinée*": in 1068, local barons and Normans began the long series of pillagings that eventually ruined the abbey so that of the present church (completed in 1165) only the apsidal chapels, the *barlong* above the choir, and the bell-tower survived in 1459. What barons and civil wars had begun, a fifteenth-century abbot — "*un vandale*" exclaims Monsieur Gybal, who deplores the Gothic — completed by trying to convert Mozac to the 'flamboyant' style. Finally, absentee incumbents in the eighteenth century allowed the church to crumble. A sad story, most unusual in the Auvergne which has preserved some 250 Romanesque buildings.

I was unaware of all this when I first visited Mozac so the ugly slab-sided building came as a brutal shock. However, what sculptured capitals remain in the interior are among the most beautiful work created by twelfth-century artists. Two of them, preserved from the ambulatory, stand on the floor of the nave at the west-end and both are unusual for their subject: the first shows men gathering in the grape harvest; the second the Holy Women at the tomb of Christ, holding vials of perfume; while, on another face, there is a beautifully detailed and ingenious rendering of sleeping Roman soldiers. A few more capitals, all excellent work that brings home sharply what a loss there has been here, have survived at the east-end. The curé, a patient and saintly-looking man, will show you other great treasures: an exquisite casket of Limousin enamel-work of the twelfth century and another, of the sixteenth century, the only painted *châsse* of this kind in France. In the sacristy is the seal of Pépin le Bref used by the king to 'stamp' the relics of St Austremoine he brought from Volvic.

Finally — a bizarre detail that I did not personally check — the walls of this church are built of a calcearous stone which gives off a 'sick' smell when rubbed with the fingers. "What a symbol for the Jansenists" — writes Henri Pourrat — "for Riom was the native hearth of the Arnould, the Soanen and many others: the very church that we raise to God can never be created but out of our corrupt human nature."

Marsat, south-west of Riom, contains a celebrated example of the 'Black Virgin' image quite common in the Auvergne. A powerful rendering, this one, rather similar to the Lady at Ronzières, near Issoire, which was 'discovered' by an ox. The statue is tastefully enthroned in a chapel that shows the arms of this sixth-century priory, said to be the first Marial shrine in France. It was founded by St Priest as a refuge for widows and unmarried girls.

The treatment of the robes is most elegant and the Virgin has a sad, sensitive, brooding face that one does not easily forget. She is the subject of a pilgrimage the first Sunday after Ascension when the people from Riom carry here 'the wheel of wax' — originally three kilometres long, the exact distance from that town to Marsat — offered as thanksgiving for deliverance from Norman raiders. The village is pretty, although it has suffered from the emigration to which these 'Limagne' villages were so prone in the late nineteenth and early twentieth centuries; for, when the families left, the houses crumbled.

The third church, that of Ennezat on the Maringues road east of Riom, is quite different in style. The body of the church, which is Romanesque, is built of the mellow, honey-brown arkhose I mentioned earlier; the choir, the ambulatory and the apsidal chapels are Gothic, of the sombre Volvic stone. This is a handsome, spacious building noted for its fifteenth-century frescoes portraying The Last Judgment and the meeting in limbo of the living — mystically speaking — and the dead. The Romanesque capitals are worth examining: one of them shows the usurer, his money bag at his feet, firmly grasped by the arms by two virile figures who obviously intend him no good at all. The church, which contains several other interesting things, perhaps owed its late medieval prosperity to the richness of the black soil hereabouts. The district is known as the 'Marais' (a corruption of *les Jardins de maraîchers* — the gardens of vegetable-growers) and its drainage in recent years has made of it some of the best farming land in the Auvergne.

North of Riom this triangle of country — roughly framed by the straight, fast Gannat-Vichy road, and by the prettier undulating N. 493 that passes through the Forest of Randan on its way to Vichy — contains many interesting things. From the point of view of landscape it is not exciting, yet by no means tame, and the birch and larchwoods of the Forêt de Randan are delightful picnicking grounds at any time between May and the end of October. Randan itself is a pretty village scarcely more than an adjunct to the wooded park of the burnt-out château, destroyed it is said by a cigarette carelessly left burning by a woman. Through the gates one can just make out the sad, gaunt shell of the building, once the *maison de retraite* of the favourite unmarried sisters of Louis XV. Women, apparently, played a large part of its history; one of them was a sister of Pico della Mirandola, the Renaissance philosopher. Sheep now graze in the park and there are farm buildings; but it has an abandoned, desolate air. The Italian-Renaissance influence on France also crops up at Aigueperse where Ghirlandaio painted in the church. But the Mantegna has vanished, transferred to the Louvre. On a knoll above the town, off the Randan road, once stood the most celebrated castle of the Auvergne, belonging to the Montpensier family whose name is borne by the hamlet at its foot. Not a stone of this remains. On the other side of Aigueperse, quite concealed behind a clump of trees that have grown along the bluff on which its outer walls once stood, is the Château de la Roche, the seat of the Arnoux de la Maison Rouge. This can be visited. A reticent, sun-faded old warrior now, and shorn of the curtain walls, its towers look across open country to the 'Chaîne des Volcans.' The castle was formerly one of the important strongholds of Bourbon power in the Auvergne. The famous name connected with it is that of Michel de l'Hôpital, the sixteenth-century Chancellor to whom Ronsard dedicated an ode. More importantly, he has gone down in history as one of the few truly disinterested men of his age; for he tried to hold the balance between Protestant and Catholic at the Valois court and was duly assassinated for his pains.

Near here are Artonne and St Myon, for me the most attractive villages in this part of the world. The former, especially, couched on its hill above an ambling stream, like a golden-brown cat dormant in the sun, has a huge church, all that remains of the abbey around which, no doubt, this large settlement grew. One can imagine few more pleasant places to retire to. St Myon lies in the plain, closer to the same stream: its church, also Romanesque but in a purer, more bucolic style, is worth a glance. Even more interesting is the taller, more upstanding church at Thuret, on the main Randan-Vichy road. Here, the sculptured capitals and corbel ends, fascinatingly archaic, are early sketches for the richly humanist carvings at Mozac, Issoire and in Notre-Dame-du-Port at Clermont. Do not, however, if the weather should be gloomy, try to illuminate the church as I did by standing on a chair to attach a likely-looking plug to a neighbouring point: there was a foray of sparks, a slightly pungent odour that might have offended St Amable, and I found myself sprawled among the chairs, more astonished than hurt. Fortunately the curé was not about. The French are apt to be casual where electrics are concerned.

Lastly, there is Effiat — surely the most *campagnard* and unpretentious of all the châteaux of the Basse-Auvergne. No re-shaped medieval fortress this, but a steeproofed mansarded domestic retreat so secluded behind tall elms and beeches I passed it twice without realising it was there. The first time I called, I was brusquely informed by a lined, moutachioed old face, framed in the casement window, that, the time being 11.30, I would of course understand that lunch was in preparation. On the second occasion I realised this had been the Marquis himself; jacketed *à l'anglais*, dignified but precise and firm on points of detail, he looks not at all like the plump-cheeked crisp-bearded grandee, Antoine Coeffier, Marshal of France, who built the place in 1625, the better to enjoy his retirement. Alas! as the guide-book on these "Châteaux Vivants" sadly notes, ". . . the

Marshal will not live to see the work achieved". The place is better known for its association with his second son, the Marquis of Cinq-Mars, favourite of the ambivalent, close-natured Louis XIII. Too many honours at too green an age turned this young man's head: he became involved in plots composed by older and more cynical men. Others confessed too freely and Cardinal Richelieu took his opportunity to get rid of a potentially dangerous enemy. The young man, only twenty-two, was executed at Lyon. "Perverted by a debauched court" says the caption beneath his portrait: perhaps. The face above the high, elaborate lace collar of the time is that of a dandy, the mouth sensual, the eyes hooded — he knew what he was doing. Since then, the great house has mellowed quietly into an arboreal somnolence. The interiors are pleasingly domestic and the garden behind, with its pool and raised walk, makes an amiable resting-place on a hot day.

III

CLERMONT-FERRAND

Clermont — *Clarus Mons*: the 'bright mountain' must have been the Puy-de-Dôme, some 5,000 feet high. From the centre of the city it is seen only briefly as one tops the Boulevard Lafayette by the black and white eighteenth-century sobriety of the Hôtel-Dieu, built to shelter the poor and the sick. Otherwise, thickly wooded hills above medicinal Royat intervene. The Puy is an excellent weather gauge at all seasons. If it remains free of cloud during the morning, the weather is likely to be fine all day; but if, towards midday, its crest — in shape and colour rather like a grand plum pudding, tipped with white sauce all winter — should be assailed with grey cloud, rain or snow are in the offing. Normally, it rains very little here in winter; while in the hills, my predominating impression is of clear blue sky and biting cold. But the weather in Clermont can change with disconcerting rapidity: one night a drop of 30 degrees was recorded, and this in mid-summer.

The name was given only in Roman times. The Gauls, a Celtic people who settled in the mountains to the south 300 years before Christ, called it Nemaussos. When the Romans came they stayed, liking the place for its healing waters (fine houses with mosaic floors have been traced below the Boulevard Desaix and the rue d'Assas, off the central Place de Jaude). Descending from the Hôtel-Dieu, past the functional propriety of the Faculty of Medicine and turning right by a cinema that rarely shows any but the most improper films, one enters this main square, whose garden — a sandy oblong, the conversational refuge of under-employed Algerians — is nicely terminated by two statues. The rearing horseman is Vercingétorix, Gaulois hero of Julius Caesar's time; the sternly pointing figure is that of General Desaix, also native-born, who was killed at Marengo some 1,800

years later. With a little imagination one can suppose the
latter — a most successful soldier — to be saying to
Vercingétorix, "Ah! my friend, if only you had not ridden off so
wildly into Burgundy, Gaul might have been saved from the
Romans".

For, in fact, Vercingétorix took advantage of an over-
confident Roman general to drive the invaders out of central
Auvergne. The battle took place on the 'Plateau de Gergovie'
whose escarpment drops sharply to the 'Limagne' above the main
road to Issoire. At first the battle went to the Romans but
Vercingétorix, rallying his troops, threw in his reserves at the
vital moment and ran the enemy down the hill towards La
Roche-Blanche. What is more he restrained his casqued,
moustachioed warriors from their customary furious pursuit and
so won the day. Unfortunately, the rest of the campaign turned
out badly. Although he had succeeded, for the first and only
time, in uniting the various Celtic tribes under his own
command, Vercingétorix forsook his mountain fastness (where a
later imperialism, in World War II, also had difficulty with the
local maquisards) and went north into Burgundy where he was
trapped, besieged, and eventually surrendered to avoid the
massacre of his followers. Caesar, after displaying his noble
captive in a 'triumph', had him strangled in the prison of
Tullianum (Tulles, in the Corrèze). The scene of the battle makes
a pleasant trip, and one can only wonder, looking down the hill,
how the Romans dared attack a strongly fortified encampment
up such a steep slope. The best approach is through Ceyrat along
the D.21. This road winds through orchards and market gardens
in the trough between the twin *puys* of Montrognon and Giroux.

Below the latter is Opmé, with a great square-towered castle
occupied in 1940, after the fall of France, by another famous
soldier, Marshal de Lattre de Tassigny. Here he reformed the
cadres of a new French army in the camp he had built, with
extraordinary speed, on the opposite slope (it is now the campus
of what we should call a College of Further Education).

While in this charming suburban area of Clermont it would
be a pity to miss La Bâtisse, between Opmé and Chanonat, for
this sandstone castle, shyly tucked away — it is quite hidden by
trees — on a narrow ledge above the little river Auzon, is a gem
of its kind, an object lesson in how to contrive, in a minimum

of space, a delightful ambiance of garden and water. Quite why anyone should have built a medieval fortress in such a secluded valley it is difficult to understand unless it was to guard the approach to Chanonat, which once had an important Benedictine monastery and a *commanderie* of the Knights Templar of St John. At any rate, of the original thirteenth-century castle only the east wing and two towers survive; the drawbridge over the stream and the curtain-walls disappeared when the eighteenth-century south wing and the gardens (as we see them now) were created by the second generation of the Girard family; bankers who achieved nobility, and the means to purchase Le Bâtisse, in the person of Jean, who became Secretary "to the King, house and crown of France" in 1696. It was his son and grandsons who had the gardens so prettily arranged in the style of Le Nôtre.

One enters the grounds by the main gate, past the little family chapel, and a gravel drive leads directly into the rose-garden. To the right is the medieval wing — terminating in a fat round tower capped by a perky dome on stilts — to which the later buildings are joined by another, casement-windowed tower. To the left, the upper garden ends in an embrasured wall looking across the stream to another garden whose 'walk' is punctuated by a tiny folly: this arbour, discreetly veiled, was once the scene — or so the jaunty, moustached guide likes to hint — of amorous adventure.

To the right again, beyond an aviary, the most recently built wing looks down upon a long, narrow lawn, bordered by the stream, so contrived as to lead the eye towards the landscape designer's *chef d'oeuvre* — a lovely waterfall tumbling over stone emplacements at three levels. Now somewhat overgrown by trees, this set-piece was only part of an elaborate plan of channelled water, formal garden and shaded walks in the heyday of the castle in the late eighteenth century. Its present, wilder state adds an elegiac note to the ambiance of rustic bridge, fountains and trim terraced garden below the deep-fawn walls of the castle.

The interior, domestically charming rather than grand, is full of interesting things; but the guide is so informative it would be superfluous to go into detail except to say that the Impressionist paintings of Jean de Chasteauneuf, the last of the Girard line, are excellent work of a really talented 'minor' painter. He died without issue in 1961 and La Bâtisse passed, by a previous marriage, into the family of Arnoux de la Maison-Rouge, which also owns the Château de la Roche, near Aigueperse. The present owner, himself a distinguished soldier, had the misfortune to lose his elder son, an officer of the Legion, killed in Algeria in 1959. Happily, there are other children, for one gathers he has spent a great deal of time and money in restoring the house.

There is one amusing story attached to it. In 1791, local republicans got wind that Monsieur de la Bâtisse might be harbouring priests on the run. Bursting in, they were received by Monsieur, sword in hand, who calmly and sternly demanded their business. While the parley went on, seven priests found the opportunity to scurry off into the countryside. The castle almoner, however, was so frightened he chose to leave by a second-storey window; and he survived, thanks to a newly-dug flower bed which broke his fall! Hauled with a rope round his neck to the fortress-prison at La Crest, he apparently survived that too, while the family — unusually — went unpunished.

No other great castle except Châteaugay remains in the vicinity of Clermont. On the whole its historical past, though eventful enough in a minor sort of way, does not obtrude upon the modern city, which is functional, architecturally inoffensive, efficiently run. Clermont, as opposed to Montferrand, is more administrative than industrial and the professional classes who work for the *Département*, for Michelin and for the rapidly growing university live for the most part in the upper suburbs of Chamalières, Royat and Durtol. The white hope of the moderate Right in French politics, Valéry Giscard d'Estaing — now President of France — was mayor of Chamalières for several years. Originally there were two separate cities, one on each commanding rise, and Clermont and Montferrand existed as such, in a state of inactive hostility, throughout the Middle Ages. It was Catherine de Médici — her mother came of the locally powerful de la Tour d'Auvergne family — who, through her conniving, active influence, eventually assured the supremacy of Clermont.

The union was haggled over throughout the seventeenth century and finally effected in 1731, so that the social and cultural life of the place became centred on Clermont. Monferrand came back into its own in the late nineteenth century when the brothers Michelin took over a factory that had specialised in macintoshes and small rubber goods. They perceived the growing importance of the motor-car, and the contemporary evidence of their success in cornering the tyre-market is the immense sprawl of factories that dominates Montferrand. Michelin, though paternalistic and sternly resisting any signs of trade-union militance — there were riots in the thirties at the time of the *Front Populaire* — is a go-ahead firm. The comparative quietness of the Paris Métro is due to their development of a tyre suitable for underground trains. Since World War II they have expanded enormously, securing financial liaison with both Pirelli and Citröen, and one hears disparaging mutters in Clermont of the firm's economic omniscience and of its political influence. The fact remains that the city's extremely rapid development during the last ten years, with a population steadily approaching 200,000, has been largely due to Michelin's industrial acumen. The fine rugby stadium is named after the family while a new sports and recreational centre near St Alyre, once the site of a famous monastery, doubtless owes something to their support.

Now, further developments are in active preparation along the *route nationale* leading out to Riom. One can only hope that the industrial housing will be planned in a more elegant style than that which already exists in the residential suburbs of Montferrand. From what I have observed in other parts of central France, there are plenty of excellent examples of modern housing development to copy; it would be a pity if such a fine environment were spoiled by any greedy haste to expand at all costs.

For the visitor there is plenty of good and relatively cheap accommodation. The two great churches are certianly worth seeing. The black, Gothic one which towers over the old quarter was begun in 1248 by an ambitious bishop who, presumably, wished it to rival the splendid early Gothic achievements in the Ile de France. Personally, I find it oppressive, one of those buildings - like the huge red-brick basilica of Toulouse — whose very massive, unyielding quality somehow diminishes their religious atmosphere. But there are some beautiful stained-glass windows in the apse, best seen in the light of the early morning sun, and a Jacquemart clock whose complexity makes one marvel at the ingenuity of late medieval craftsmen.

The Place de la Victoire, opening out on the cathedral's southern flank, was the scene of the most significant event in the modern history of the Auvergne, the so-called 'Grands Jours' of 1665. This curious public trial is worth a short digression because it marks the turning-point in the life of the whole region.

We, in England, were extremely fortunate that a strong dynastic line, the Tudors, enabled our developing nation to pass, with comparatively little social conflict or civil war, from the feudal to a steadily evolving and broadly-based society in which a politically conscious merchant-class both supplemented and restrained that aristocracy upon whose stability, or otherwise, the feudal system had always depended. Kings might come and kings might go but the landed barons survived, a restive nucleus of potential disorder if the royal authority were weak. The French people were not so lucky: the disorder was not potential but all-pervasive and chronic, a sort of fever that died down in one part of the body of France only to spring up in another. In the end the aristocratic order had to be broken by sheer violence, the echoes of which still reverberate in the background of French politics to this day. Throughout the Middle Ages and well into the seventeenth century, civil violence was the rule. France is a large country and the king's authority simply did not extend to outer provinces like the Auvergne except in the rare intervals of peace between internal or external wars.

The Hundred Years' War was an especially disturbed period, for even when English Plantagenet and French Valois had momentarily — through financial exhaustion or dynastic preoccupation — agreed not to fight each other, their unemployed soldiers continued to pillage and brawl. They had to live somehow, which meant, in effect, off the people whose lands they had 'occupied'. The king himself had no standing army so he had to rely on the most powerful branch of the local nobility to maintain law and order. Such families — the Mercoeur, the de la Tour d'Auvergne, the Bourbon, the Polignac in the Velay and the Forez, were so mutually jealous of each other's power as to be quite heedless of civil order. Upon these larger predators depended other minor ones, inter-marrying, carving out new alliances, adapting to the balance of power as it changed from decade to decade, often from year to year. Which is why one can scarcely travel ten miles without spotting some crag-top eyrie, time-riven and weathered as an old decaying oak the years cannot quite kill; or a splendidly preserved shell, its outer walls virtually intact, like Léotoing above the Alagnon near the Issoire-Massiac road. In such strongholds brigand succeeded baron till the two were virtually indistinguishable.

So bad did this state of affairs become that for long periods in the fourteenth century and part of the fifteenth — and again during the Religious Wars of the mid-sixteenth — commerce almost ceased. What produce there was the local war-lord stole, burned or appropriated as his legal due. Hence 'les patis', a form of protection by which the peasant ceded most of his crop 'voluntarily' to avoid having all of it seized. The same applied to townships like St Flour and Brioude, which bought off their marauders only, quite often, to be later accused by king or royal governor of having collaborated with the 'enemy'. Yet what else could the elders, or consuls, do if they were to survive?

Once the English had finally abandoned all claim to the throne of France and the religious quarrel had been temporarily settled, (Henry of Navarre having renounced his faith to become Catholic King of France) some sort of royal authority was restored. And then hour found the man in Cardinal Richelieu, a politician, Louis XIII remarked, "ready to set fire to the four corners of my realm", whom he at first refused to appoint to his council. Very soon the King had to accept him, and Richelieu went to the heart of the problem. Traditionally, no land could be held without proven legal title and Richelieu enforced this; while all castles of purely military purpose, save those under the direct control of the king, were ruthlessly pulled down: Montpensier, whose duke commissioned the Mantegna now in the Louvre, is one outstanding example, Mercoeur, off the road to Ardes-sur-Couze, another. Louis XIV continued the policy but since unruly country nobles, known as *hobereaux*, and too idle or too wary to seek employment at his court, continued to misbehave, he eventually lost patience and established the travelling plenary court which sat in judgement on the Place de la Victoire. Its declared purpose was to hear any and every complaint against the lesser nobility.

It would be pleasant to record that all the evildoers met their just deserts. Unfortunately, word that the King meant business this time had gone forth. The Vicomte de la Mothe-Canillac of whom a chronicler records with conscious irony that he had "killed only three men" was tried, condemned and executed the same day; but his more powerful relative from Pont-du-Château, the Marquis de Canillae — a man of outstanding arrogance and cruelty — and Gaspard d'Espinchal, lord of Massiac, whose career we shall hear about later, both fled abroad, as did many others. It is said of Montboissier, one nobleman on the list, that he watched the whole proceedings from an upstairs window in a house opposite, smiled a saturnine smile and, next day, quietly rode away to Spain, to die peacefully in his bed.

Several streets in this quarter record the names of seventeenth- and eighteenth-century governors — notably Trudaine and Boulainvilliers — who tried to restore prosperity to the Basse-Auvergne once the 'Grands Jours' had firmly established royal authority. But bad communications and the dominance of 'Paris' government — two things of which the local press still complains — crippled their efforts. Very often these men went on to higher posts in the administration, for it was said that a man who could govern the Auvergne could govern any province. Certainly, well into the nineteenth century, the people here had a reputation for intractability. This is hardly surprising. Racial memory of persecution and callous government dies hard. Men of proud and independent stamp, and the Auvergnat has both these qualities to a fault, are apt to prefer going it alone if history and circumstance have taught them this is the only way to survive. Such tenacity also breeds conservatism, in the sense that a small farmer whose family has laboured generations to achieve a modest prosperity does not lightly risk what he has so hardly gained merely for the sake of change. Gachon, a sympathetic observer who knows these people, remarks that the Auvergnat would rather continue than innovate. He sums up this whole matter with cryptic wisdom: "The Auvergnat suffered too much, struggled too much. Suddenly he perceived his misery, his too great numbers. His hunger for land became transformed by the need for a life less brutal . . ." Hence the steady depopulation of many villages throughout the nineteenth century.

Now, of necessity, the Auvergnat has come to terms with his world: he remains tenacious, holds and improves his land, builds fine modern houses of remarkably pleasant design that blend well with the landscape because constructed with local materials. Phylloxera ruined the vineyards in the late nineteenth century, and wine production no longer forms a major part of his living; market-gardening, fruit-farming and forage-crops have replaced viniculture. However, many small farmers still produce their own wine, and the *vin du pays* from the commercial vineyards, usually classified V.D.Q.S., makes pleasant drinking (the red is better than the rosé, except for that known as *Rosé de Corent*).

So much for the cathedral and its rather banal 'place' on which history, if not changed, was at least diverted for the good of the people. The streets that climb to it from the Avenue des Etats-Unis contain a portal here, a balustraded staircase there, several emblazoned courtyards that bear witness to the days when such houses — now tenements or workshops — were the homes of bankers, notably the Chauchat and the Gayte, who financed kings in the fifteenth century. Among these, the Musée Fontfreyde is worth half an hour if you like genre pictures of local events and local worthies, while the furniture, also of local provenance, is often admirably made. This quarter, however, has sadly declined; it is now almost a slum and wears the shamefaced look of decayed gentility. The same must be said of the old part of Monferrand, around the black-stone church once — astonishingly, in view of its size — merely the chapel of the seignurial fortress. A great pity, for the stone carving on the Maison du Sire de Beaujeu, the Maison des Centaures and the Maison de Lucrèce is highly elegant. The cultural authority should look to both these areas; their present crumbling state does little credit to a well-to-do municipality.

No-one should leave Clermont without seeing its principal monument, the Romanesque basilica of Notre Dame du Port, off the rue du Port leading downhill behind the Hôtel de Ville to the Place Delille. Unhappily, this fine church is so placed in a hollow, below the present level of the streets, as to be invisible in the round. The Revolutionaries pulled down its tower and defaced the *tympan* over the main door. The nineteenth-century restorer (not Viollet-le-Duc, who completed the Gothic cathedral) made a sad hash of the tower and replaced the native grey *lauze* tiles, which weather so handsomely, with slabs of Volvic slate. But the carvings on the apse are intact, and the geometrical patterns of the several-coloured stone decoration round the roof and the apsidal chapels subtly lighten the carefully proportioned masses of the east end. This mosaic decoration, a unique feature of Auvergne Romanesque, is found on all the big churches and most of the smaller ones of the period.

Inside, the majestic proportions of nave, choir and apse are at once impressive. Yet this is a building one needs to visit several times. I must admit I did not fully appreciate the architect's -superb treatment of space and mass, still less the delicate variation in the colour of his stone, until I chanced to go in one evening while Mass was being held. Truthfully, the natural light is seldom good enough for the interior to be seen as a whole. But the capitals of the choir can be illuminated and they are remarkable enough to be worth several visits — sermons in stone for the simple people of the twelfth century who could not read nor, presumably, understand the spoken Latin in which the bible-stories might be told. Since these sculptures are repeated, with slight variations, in all the great Romanesque churches of the region, and can be seen better at St Nectaire, Issoire and Brioude, I shall not attempt to describe them here. But do not miss the Annunciation, the Resurrection of the Virgin, with its rapt male faces brooding over the Holy Mystery; and the unexpectedly earthy 'Expulsion from Eden' in which Adam seems to be aiming a kick at the supine author of his 'fall'.

At the bottom of the rue du Port, the popular shopping street of the city and the haunt of busy urban housewives and their country cousins in search of the odd bargain (there are some good antique shops in the neighbouring lanes), is the Place Delille. This is called after a local abbé known for his lyric poetry — rather saccharine-sweet for my taste. In this square, where Peter the Hermit preached the First Crusade and Urban II blessed those departing on it, is a good sixteenth-century fountain and a great deal of traffic. Beyond lies industrial dereliction and an *aggroupement* — the ugly word exactly fits them — of supermarkets on the road east to Thiers. This is the only really unsightly suburb of Clermont-Ferrand. Hurry through it.

Royat, at the opposite end of the city, is a distinctly attractive example of how a formerly independent community can be 'adopted' into a city without losing too much of its individual identity.

"And so to Royat, its gaseous springs and its whiffy caves, its chocolate-making and its amethyst cutting," writes Henri Pourrat, with his usual bubble; and goes on to remark that it is 'all embroidered and re-embroidered, pinnacled and pointed, golden ornament upon golden ornament'. Very much so, for the little spa — after falling into such desuetude over the centuries that travellers remarked upon its squalor — came to splendid renewal in the mid-nineteenth century when the Empress Eugénie made it fashionable again and the *beau monde* descended in great numbers to cure themselves of gout, arthritis, and the effects of high living. Huge hotels in Second-Empire décor, fawn, beige and white, turretted, mansarded, and highly expensive, overlook the charming central garden with its arboreal walks, café-terrace, bijou shops, thermal baths and casino. Lesser breeds without the capital rent bed-sitting rooms in Chamalières or in the upper part of the town, walking slowly up (or down) to take their daily dose of carboniferous water, which tastes disgusting and possibly accounts for the profusion of sweet-shops and their consoling 'gooey' products. These oddly resemble, in colour at least, the pink, green, aquamarine and purple volcanic stones which local industry cuts and polishes as — conceivably — mementoes mori. The place is also full of 'grottes' which I was careful not to visit as they bore me, especially when they contain rock facsimiles of alsatian dogs. Though it is only fair to record that the literary and classically-minded Bishop Fénelon took one of them as his model for the Cave of Calypso: an unlikely tale that may be true.

Certainly, Royat (Rubiacum to the Romans because the rock and the soil are so red) is romantic in a raffiné, Second-Empire style. The *jeunesse dorée* of Clermont frequent its cafes, when the weather permits them to sit outside, to comment upon who has seduced whom and whether Patrick has met his match, at last, in Marie-Claude . . .

Climb the winding hill out of the hotel quarter, whose several hairpins are a constantly accepted challenge to Porsche, Alfa-Romeo and the sportier Mercedes-Benz, and a more contemporary elegance prevails. Even the tower blocks are white and dazzling, set off by villa-gardens luxuriant with flowers. Truly charming, and unselfconsciously so, is the little Parc Bargoin at the very top of the hill, whose clipped lawns and curving paths — following the easier contours of its bowl-like hollow — aristocratically tall trees and precise flower arrangements are just the place to beguile an hour after lunch. Or for a discreet assignment.

Taking the other direction — to the right, at the top of the Boulevard Bazin — one reaches the old town, less spic-and-span but with a weathered and more retiring charm. Narrow lanes lead into the Place Cohendy where stands the eleventh-century Eglise St Léger, half castle, half church, which the abbots of Mozac fortified against the assaults of local barons. Not a beautiful building by any means, but it has two fine thirteenth-century rose-windows and a tenth-century crypt. From here one may look across the deep ravine hollowed out by the river Tiretaine to the opposite spur, called 'Le Paradis', where a rugged manor-house has been converted into a hotel. From here there is a splendid view over Royat and Chamalières. The road from the belvedere soon narrows into a lane, the Chemin des Crètes which leads up through woods to Villars and eventually to Fontanes and the cross-roads at the foot of the Puy-de-Dôme. It is a delightful walk at any time but particularly so in autumn, for the trees in the valley below are nearly all beeches and chestnuts.

The Place de Jaude, when it was a marshy place (watered by the Tiretaine) and fringed with willows, had a temple to Jove: at the very top of the Puy-de-Dôme was a temple to Mercury, the messenger god of trade. Scarcely anything remains of this Roman splendour, built of rich marble from Pentelicon and Thebes, and of the red stone of Paros in the Aegean Sea, and nothing at all of the Mercury carved by Zenodorus — "a colossus of bronze that demanded ten years labour and cost millions of sesterces". Instead, there is an observatory and a slender fretwork of television-mast: "*Austres temps, autres moeurs*".

Leave the car on the grassy open space behind the inn near the top of the Col de Ceyssat and climb the plainly-marked path through the pine-woods to the top of the Puy: it gives one an appetite for lunch and the prospect, south-west across the 'Chaîne des Volcans', is tremendous.

IV

EASTERN HILLS AND VALLEY CASTLES

A straight, fast road — the *route nationale* to Lyon — hastens the traveller from Clermont to Lezoux. Soon afterwards this road begins to wind as it climbs the escarpment above the river Dore until Thiers, perched precipitously like a Mediterranean hilltown on an out-lying spur of the Monts du Forez, comes fully into view.

To the south of this road lie the *pays découpés* — rolling hill country brought into cultivation by those small farmers who were awarded it when the big landed estates were broken up during the first years of the Revolution. Yet, as so often in the Auvergne, paradox rears its engaging head: first, there are so many castles in this small area the stranger rubs his eyes and wonders whether he is not going round in circles, seeing the same place from different aspects; secondly, although the land is obviously fertile, some of the villages contain crumbling, abandoned houses. I can find no explanation for the first anomaly except that this *is* very pleasant country in which to have a castle (those in the high mountains look romantic but must be piercingly bleak in midwinter). Many of these small castles were purchased by the new nobility of the post-Napoleonic era, while a few slipped back into the hands of their former owners. Others have been rescued from dereliction by bankers or industrialists and restored as summer *plaisances*. Only one, Ravel, has a really well documented past. It belonged to the d'Estaing family and can be visited. Most of those intact are strictly private; but Codignat has recently become a hotel, a fate increasingly common for châteaux of modest size.

The second point is easily explained: the farms in these parts are too small to support large families so younger sons have been forced to emigrate to Paris, Clermont or wherever work is available. The mechanisation of the twentieth century has naturally hastened this process, since more machines mean fewer hands. Inevitably, therefore, when old people died or whole families left for the cities, houses crumbled for want of tenants. Happily, the process no longer continues and urban folk in need of a week-end villa often buy up and renovate such houses.

Pont-du-Château, the first small town on the *route nationale*, will not detain the visitor although it has a good, early Gothic church and some fine views over the Allier. It has always been important for its bridge. The present eighteenth-century one took so long to build that the 'Intendant' had to threaten the masons with legal action over their dilatoriness. The strategic castle, now destroyed, was held by that Montboissier who watched himself burnt in effigy in Clermont during the *'Grands Jours'*. His twelve household ruffians, known as 'apostles', used to convert the recalcitrant with sticks and stones. That Montboissier's subjects were resentful is hardly surprising for he taxed them four times: once for himself, once for his wife, again for his children, and lastly for the king. Now, Pont-du-Château is a Sunday resort for the people of Clermont who use the broad stretch of water on the town side of the bridge for swimming and sailing.

At Chignon, unless you are in a great hurry to get to Thiers, turn sharp right for Chauriat, a large village that has prospered, of recent years, among its vineyards. The church is a splendid example of country Romanesque. The exterior, crowned by a good modern tower, is handsome, the intricate, many coloured mosaic work of the south transept and the delicate treatment of the blind arcading especially fine. The interior, like that at Issoire, has been painted; which is a pity when the stone has such a rich natural colour. The double arches at the west end are a typical feature of such churches but it is the capitals that fascinate. There is a good Last Supper, a familiar theme of the period, while an endearing serpent adorns the decorative work on another column; yet another shows two archaic-innocent faces peering out of leaves, and a small naked figure, knees hunched, appears from a bunch of foliage. On the column supporting the double arch birds gnaw at a nightmarish head and, on the south side of the choir, is a highly original version of another common theme — St Michael casting down the Devil. One makes what one likes of the symbolism: it is the highly individual treatment, half nightmare, half vision, of these recurrent subjects which charms in such simple churches. Several cellars in the vicinity of the church invite you to sample the local wine.

Lezoux is rather ugly but notable for a fine red clay that attracted the Romans to establish ceramic workshops here. The modern product is not remarkable.

Thiers is certainly the place not to miss in this area. The Durolle, flowing eastwards along the valley it shares with the road to Lyon, joins the Dore just before the town as if to emphasise that its prosperity and historical development depended on the water here, which has special non-calcearous properties favouring the manufacture of fine steel and paper. The latter, however, was a victim of the large-scale industralisation of the nineteenth century. The long white building that crowns the hill on the north side of the old town is the National School of Cutlery. By car, one winds steeply up the hill to the very centre of the town, a pocket-handkerchief square with a balustraded *emplacement* offering a good view of les Margerides — wooded spurs of the Forez that hem in the town, dropping so sheer to the Durolle that the river itself cannot be seen from here.

The best way to explore Thiers is to take one of the lanes winding down from the little *place* to the big mill by the river and then climb up again by the road that borders the tumbling waters so cleverly harnessed, in the sixteenth century, to practical ends. There are, in these lanes, some delightful half-timbered houses of a kind extremely rare in this part of the world, where stone is the dominant material. Descending by the rue Pirou and the rue des Rochers one notices several, mostly in good repair — the best is the 'House of the Seven Sins', so called for its elaborate, gargoyle decoration in sculpted wood. Another was the *hôtel* that sheltered François I on his return from a victorious campaign in Italy. Some of the smaller houses lower down are remarkable for their pretty, terraced gardens ingeniously making use of every square foot of available space (it is a myth that the French do not cultivate flower gardens, as the traveller in this region at once discovers). Cross the stream by the handsome, disused mill and you are on the road which leads into the open space by the old church of St Pierre Moûtier, once part of a famous abbey under the rule of Cluny. Nothing remains of the abbey except a château-like building with lopped towers and decorative wooden balconies; the church, very early Romanesque or even Carolingian, is unjustly neglected for it has some excellent foliage capitals peopled by birds and local fauna that might be man or beast; or the one evolving into the other.

From here a road climbs the hill past what might be a rather gloomy study in industrial dereliction if it were not for the leaping, babbling, cascading waters, diverted into a cross-channel here, a long calm runnel there; a small river has been, quite literally, terraced and channelled to provide water-power for the disused wooden workshops — they are scarcely factories — that once sent fine steel scissors, instruments and cutlery all over western Europe. Now they are hollow-eyed, deserted, melancholy witness to the march of progress, their little bridges broken down or barred to the visitor in case he should fall through them into the clear, bounding waters. Further up there are some modern factories, including a cutlery; but the greater part of the industry, which still produces surgical instruments and parts for cars, is now elsewhere in the town, so the workers no longer have to lie face downwards to grind their metal, with rushing water below and a dog couched obediently across their legs to keep them warm in winter! At the top of the hill, steep lanes lead off back into the town. But it is worth lingering a while to admire, along the thickly wooded slopes on the opposite side of the hill, modern villas in white, green and blue nestling into the trees. Despite its abandoned workshops there is nothing desolate about Thiers. Happily so, for its situation is superb, aloft on this balcony-like escarpment which looks right across the broadest part of the 'Limagne' to the rounded masses of the 'Chaîne des Volcans', and southwards to the higher peaks of the Monts-Dore — blue-black outlines against a background of gently moving cloud or, if the weather is stormy, hazy and mist-wreathed, re-emergent from time to time like rocky ogres in battle with the elements.

Thiers, in spite of its strategic position, has witnessed no great events. But its people have a reputation for fierce independence and for loyalty to the small craft-communities their skills fostered. In the sixteenth and seventeenth centuries they created a communal, patriarchal way of life in which all duties were shared and any surplus produce was given to the poor. Such a township, one might fancy, could easily take to Protestantism. In

Puy de la Vache and Puy de Lassolas

Puy de Sancy

Château de Tournoël

Château de Chazeron

Notre Dame du Port, Clermont; tympan over south door

The Cathedral; Clermont

Royat; La Source Eugénie

Thiers; Maison du Pirou, sixteenth century

Thiers; bridge over the Durolle

Thiers; Cutler at work

Medieval paper-making at the mill of Richard le Bas above Ambert

Ruined fortress of Mauzun

La Bourboule and la Chaîne du Sancy

Interior of Château d'Aultéribe

fact, this was one of the towns in which the heresy took root: Maringues, across the plain towards Riom, was another. An active band of *Réformistes* beat a small Catholic army on the hill at Cognat in 1568 and later sacked Thiers when the Catholic governor refused to open its gates. Yet a contemporary traveller describes it as "a highly commercial city, stoutly built and populous, well-known for paper making, knives and playing cards", while Henri III confirmed its royal charter when he passed through fifteen years later. Evidently religious broils did not interrupt the trading. And, oddly enough, the villages in the countryside around Thiers were famous for loyalty to their priests on the run during the persecutions of the atheistic phase of the Revolution.

To describe a landscape as idyllic is to risk being labelled *faux-naif*. The hills called Les Bois Noirs, north of Thiers, are — nevertheless — idyllic. Their highest point, the Puy Snidre at 3,700 feet, is not remarkably high as this region goes; but the sense of remoteness, of a rural life that continues quietly, steadfastly to pursue its unselfconscious way soon takes a hold on the traveller who is prepared to amble, stop for half an hour, and amble on again when and where the mood takes him. The main road to Châteldon is pleasant but apt to be crowded at weekends since it is the through road to Vichy and the gastronomic pleasures of that amiable, beflowered and Pétain-haunted spa. An alternative takes you along the right bank of the Dore through Dorat, which has pretensions to becoming a holiday-centre and a church, on a grassy rise, with the most quaintly machicolated tower in the Auvergne; a nineteenth-century church architect's 'folly'. It also affords the best approach via Puy-Guillaume to Châteldon, the nearest thing, in its pastoral, self-contained and mildly prosperous seclusion, to a Cotswold village *à l'Auvergne*. A stream shaded by an avenue of limes unhurriedly guides you into the *bourg*, which proves to be even more enticing than it looks from a distance: lanes diverge with pleasing irrelevance between half-timbered houses lacy with ramblers and murmurous with bees, while the stream continually divides to run beneath or around the houses and reappear below the next street. There is even a fourteenth-century *tour d'horloge* with a musical chime, while one workshop-entrance mysteriously reverberates with the sound of rushing waters. The place is known for ebony-carving but of this I found no evidence. The church has a good Crucifixion and some unusually fine Baroque statues.

The castle, teasingly glimpsed from the road into the village, completely disappears behind its magnificent trees as one climbs towards it: a very grand and private place one may not visit. Local historians are silent about Châteldon and no-one seems to know about it. Long may it remain secluded from the mainstream of this life, dormant among its rivulets whose bridges invite one idly to lean and think of nothing at all. Some five miles above the town, near Pont de Ris, the Dore, which has flirted some time with the broader Allier, finally joins it.

Ris itself — off the main road — is another sleepy place whose inhabitants viewed me with some astonishment before resuming their pre-lunch conversations: they would probably treat a visitor from Mars in the same way. From the Châteldon road one gets a first view of the village slumbering in its hollow: a château with a square, double-windowed tower dominates the foreground to the right; a cluster of deep-brown-stone houses, roofs of rust-coloured tiles, the two turrets of an older ruined castle form the background, and an ordered confusion of vineyards and tiny gardens occupies the hill. The church, all that remains of a celebrated priory, is the very prototype of Romanesque, tall and barrel-naved with the half-barrel side aisles which proclaim an eleventh-century builder to whom the cross-ribbed supporting vault was, as yet, unknown.

From Ris, Michelin 73 offers a network of small roads into the Bois Noirs, any one of which is an enchantment on a fine, early summer day. The road to la Guillermie proposes — suddenly, as the high banks on either side give way — a view to the north-east so rich in broom that the whole landscape seems one single splendour of old-gold and pale green; there are few conifers until one climbs into the thick, silent pinewoods of the uplands. From here the enquirer-out of churches will certainly wish to continue north, through Ferrières, where russet-tiled roofs abruptly change to a glistening dark-blue, and Le Mayet. This open, rolling country, sparsely populated but closely farmed, brings him to Châtel-Montagne, a tiny wind-swept village of four main streets with a huge, Romanesque church. Here the Burgundian style meets the Auvergnat to achieve a tough simplicity that makes its effect almost without ornament, except for the eye-brow like decoration of the capitals in the apse. This rigorous purity is largely due to the hardness of the granite, which echoes that of the surrounding country. The ambulatory and the austere west porch were built about 1150 and, rather later, the walls were heightened to accommodate the triforium. Gybal, the chief authority on Avergnat Romanesque, notices the hollows of shade created by the blank arches opening onto the porch — a necessary element in a sun-lit country. This village, owing its existence to a Benedictine abbey under the rule of Cluny, stands at the tip of the Monts de la Madeleine, themselves the last spur of the Forez range forming the eastern lateral of our region. Beyond lies Burgundy.

Alternatively, one may branch east from la Guillermie over the Col du Beau Louis towards la Prugne and St Priest where uranium is now mined. Here a beautiful road strikes directly for the Puy de Montoncel at the very heart of the Bois Noirs. Or, from la Guillermie again, there is an equally lovely road, leaving the dark, secretive heights of the Puy Snidre to the left, down to St Rémy-sur-Durolle, an admirable centre from which to explore this area. From its main square there is a glimpse of the Puy-de-Dôme, massively foreboding in the hazy distance: the church occupying most of this square has been handsomely restored and offers, among other things, a fresco-life of St Rémy. The people are hospitable and the food good. My own favourite road, however, is the D.64, from St Rémy to Arconsat and Chabreloches on the main Lyon Road. Galleons of cloud roll like a benediction across the hills, shadowing the hollows, darkening for a moment the coverts of deciduous and coniferous trees. And how judiciously the French 'mix' their trees so that every shade of green mingles in the changing light. In the fields carpets of wild flowers and herbs breathe gently in the warm sun and all one hears, apart from the friendly clatter of an occasional tractor, is the murmur of water winding briskly through some woody cleft to the valley below.

In such surroundings urban pollution is a bad dream and the use of insecticides apparently unknown. I had never realised how relatively bereft of wild flowers the English countryside had become until I came to this part of France. Moreover, while song birds are comparatively rare, magpies, jays and every kind of bird of prey abound: it is rare not to see a pair of buzzards or kites circling the sky in upland country. Once, I passed a big hawk settled on a post by the road, so close that I stopped the car. We stared — doubtless in mutual surprise — for several seconds before the bird lifted his wings and flapped lazily away.

It is about here, too, at the top of the Col St Thomas, opposite the stone monument to a Monsieur Lucien Clairet (who organised the first 'marche touristique' from Roanne to Thiers) that a local wit has erected the following sign: "Ici finit la France. Ici commence l'Auvergne."

On the south side of the R,N.89, between Thiers and Boen, begins the really high country of the Forez: we shall make a broad sickle sweep through it before descending to the upper valley of the Dore to cross the 'Limagne d'Ambert'; and then climb back over the Livradois to examine, in more detail, the château-strewn foothills around Billom with which this chapter started.

There is not, truthfully, a great deal to see in the high Forez except the countryside; but this has a grandeur only matched by the central chain of peaks extending from Clermont to the Plomb du Cantal. Because it is so wild, and relatively remote from the main transit routes followed by travellers in the Middle Ages, there are no towns of any size and few castles of note. For medieval castles were built to guard strategic highways or to prey upon those who travelled them. The finest is undoubtedly Sail-sur-Couzan which I saw, one rainy April day, through a gap in the hills and resolved instantly to visit when opportunity offered. No-one with an eye to a superb view and to grandeur in ruin should miss it. It is not easy to find; one must leave the main road just before Boen, pass through Sail itself, continue along the D.6 towards St Georges and swing right, up a steep *voie ordinaire* which goes nowhere in particular, towards the plateau as far as a sign that vaguely indicates "*château*". All this time the castle — only visible from the 'route nationale' if one looks carefully, for its stone merges into the backdrop of mountain — has been lost to view. Suddenly, at the foot of a dirt road, it rears up: a towering, weathered, reddy-brown ruin, most of the east walls and one tower still standing, the curtain walls cut off short. Yet the overall plan is still plainly readable. Strangely deserted one fine Saturday in June — until I recalled that the

French work a six-day week — the place is etched vividly in my memory: to the east a sheer drop, hundreds of feet to the Lignon gorge, with plovers or pigeons flighting like white paper against the broom-speckled cliff on the opposite side; to the south another gorge opening out, lowered over by thickly wooded cliffs and cut by the road to St Just-en-Bas and Jeansagniere, the plateau we have crossed barring the view to Pierre-sur-Haute; finally, right below the castle chapel, lies Sail, a tumble of red roofs and brown walls cuddled into a bend of the river. Only a factory off the high road slightly spoils the setting. Swallow-tail butterflies and warm herbal scents pervade the place while the grass has that crisp, springy quality only found above porous crystalline rock. Over all broods the strange, vibrant silence so striking in the high Forez, the Livradois and the craggy uplands of the Margeride. Nature reigns here, composite of sun, wind, the implacable passing of the seasons — snow all winter, rain succeeding day-long heat in high summer. Yet the castle survives — an ageing, crippled lion, perennial witness to the skill of the original builders and to the fierce marauders who extended the first enceinte. So it is quite a shock, on stepping through an archway, to come upon wooden benches, arranged in a half-circle in what used to be the great hall, and to read a notice advertising a theatre season during one week in July. I wish I had gone back. Racine's "Phèdre", in such an ambiance, might be memorable.

Again one has a wide choice of minor roads: a very pleasant one, with views opening out as one climbs, is the D. 17, leading off the N.89 to Celles. Either fork after the Col de Frissonet will bring you to a Vollore — 'Ville' or 'Montagne'. The latter is a summer holiday centre, the former more interesting for its huge, slab-walled grey château, lately rebuilt, the window-frames picked out in a crystalline stone that glistens in the sun. The stark frontage looks boldly out across the valley towards Courpierre: walk round behind it and the east side, shaded by great elms and chestnuts, shows a more private face. Vollore church, mostly fourteenth and fifteenth century, has lierne vaulting with gaily painted bosses — a veritable dictionary of armorial bearings. Most of the villages hereabouts are attractive: notably Brugeron, which has magnificent views and where the local *garagiste* ingeniously and decoratively uses old tyres as flower urns; and

Chalmazel, with a restored, inhabited castle. Beyond here, over the Col du Béal, a winter-sports centre has been created.

However, my favourite village is Augerolles, proudly built of the local granite, whose houses have a prosperous, contented look. The church, founded by the great monastery of La Chaise-Dieu on the road to Le Puy, is full of interesting things: the choir and apse are Romanesque, the nave and side aisles of the fourteenth century. The wood sculptures are so good they have been removed to the Musée de Cluny in Paris but the tower (like so many others partly destroyed, in the name of equality, at the orders of Couthon, the Auvergnat 'Consul' of the Revolution) has been decently restored. By the west door is a figure of death with an inscription that reads: "I go with measured pace to seize Emperors and Popes, Kings, gentlefolk and servants. My sickle reaches far and wide, and this shore is my emblem. At whatever day, at whatever hour you must embark in my ship of death". The cemetery, which offers a fine prospect towards Vollore, has a monument to a local family who all died in Paris — sad reminder of the times when emigration drained these villages of their youth. Now they have revived, helped by the summer tourist trade that obviously supports villages like Vertolaye, Valcivières and Job, further south.

Grandrif, seen from a bend in the Ambert — St Anthème road, so nicely perched on its little plateau in the valley, is another charming village. But the most interesting thing in these parts is the Moulin de Richard le Bas, reached by a lane branching off to the left a few kilometres from Ambert. From the early Middle Ages until the nineteenth century this valley was famous for paper making: there were some 300 mills in Ambert itself during the fifteenth, sixteenth and seventeenth centuries. Some say the original skills were brought back from China by Marco Polo and introduced into this region by pilgrims returning from Italy; others that the art came from the Near East, acquired by men who had been on the Crusades. However that may be, the visit — beginning with the little museum — is fascinating. The interior of a master craftsman's house has been recreated with imaginative allusion to all sorts of human detail: one then passes into the 'factory' itself where the ancient craft is practised; the pulp, crushed and compressed by huge wooden presses, is passed into vats for dyeing and other treatment, while

real flowers, herb petals and leaves are used to create decorative
patterns. The finished products are on sale at very reasonable
prices. Mounted, the patterned sheets make attractive wall-
decoration.

The high Forez, above 3,000 feet, is virtually uninhabited
except in summer when the shepherds go up to the *'jasseries'* to
pasture the flocks of cows whose milk produces the delicious
blue-veined cheese with a thick outer crust called *fourme d'Ambert*
or *fourme de St Anthème*. The *'jas'* (known elsewhere in the Haute
Auvergne as *'buron'*) was simply a low, thatched, one-storyed
hut in which these hardy people lived all summer through, rarely
if ever descending to their farm in the valley below; what food
they could not make for themselves was brought up to them. The
cheeses were made on the spot, hung from the roof of the *jas* or
buron to 'form' and taken down, together with the cows, on St
Martin's day, to ripen in the barns and farmhouses during the
winter. The bare tops of these hills are so criss-crossed with
rivulets that the grass grows afresh all summer, even when there
is no rain. Nowadays, the little houses are more often tiled or
wooden-roofed than thatched, while the shepherd uses the
ubiquitous Citroën or his own moped to travel up and down.
Otherwise the way of life is much the same, regardless of the
radar installations on Pierre-sur-Haute.

For those who wish, above all, for quiet the Monts du Forez
offer a great deal: the roads are good and the hotel
accommodation in the larger villages is simple but of an
increasingly high standard as plumbing and electrical installations
improve. The highlands make good walking and there is fishing
in the crystal-clear valley streams. For the nature lover, also, this
is rewarding country: he may not be lucky enough to see a
wildcat or a marten, but if he is a botanist he may find the
extremely rare types of rowan and peat-moss left over from the
glacier age: while on the Puy Montoncel, in the *Bois Noirs*, exists
a kind of moss found nowhere else in the world.

Ambert is a pleasing town: one eats well and this is always a
great recommendation so far as I am concerned. I lunched there
one dampish Good Friday and had not looked forward to
anything interesting in a Catholic town long since purged of its
heretics. However, the soup was excellent and it was followed by
two fish courses so deliciously cooked I could have wished for a

third; the cheese needs no further praise than to say it was local and various, while the pastries, too, are always good in the Auvergne. The composer Chabrier, that romantic but engaging local historian, Henri Pourrat, and Mongolfier, the pioneer balloonist, were all born hereabouts.

The town's history has one amusing tale. Merle, the most ferocious and able of the Protestant guerilla-leaders of the Religious Wars — we shall encounter his exploits all over the region — had taken the place and shot a batch of bourgeois Catholics *pour décourager les autres*. But he had no great force with him and when a sizeable Catholic army approached he felt himself in some danger. So he collected all the statues he could remove from the churches in the town, stuck helmets on their heads and placed them along the battlements. Naturally, these venerable folk did not move a muscle when shot at, whereupon the Catholics, persuaded Merle was in strength, abandoned their assault.

The church of St Jean was barely fifty years old at that time: it is perhaps the most handsome late Gothic church in the whole region, adorned with a wealth of curlicues and pinnacles, while a fine rapacity of gargoyles launches out from the corbel ends. For a 'flamboyant' church the interior is cool, austere, remarkably uncluttered, and there is a good sixteenth-century Pietà in a side-chapel. These portrayals of the Virgin mourning her Son are very common in Auvergnat churches and, of whatever period, are usually worth looking at. The town has a certain reputation for gaiety and good living — unlike Arlanc, further down the road to Le Puy, which always strikes me as dour and rather disconsolate as if mourning its vanished prosperity as a lace-making centre.

From Ambert, making one's way north, it is pleasant to follow the valley of the Dore. The main road is bordered by thickly wooded cliffs rising sharply from the right bank once the plain is left behind; or one may follow the road across the foothills of the Livradois to St Roche-Savine, which has a self-concerned, preoccupied air, an imposing church with beautiful doorways and a pâtisserie that sells delicious water-ices in unusual flavours. One historian says St Roche has connections with the Parsifal legend, a statement difficult to contest ... I have no evidence either way. Certainly the Livradois and the Forez are full of legend. Pourrat makes much of the story of Eléanore of Baffie, a village near Grandrif. She was a medieval princess who tried to bring back the Golden Age by teaching 'the good life' to the local peasantry. The local folk called her the Queen of the Livradois, and on the Suc (or Puy) de la Reine there is a slab of stone said to cover her treasure. More palpably, in the ruined monastery of Chaumont, below Marsac, archaeologists exploring the crypt found a gathering of mummified corpses arranged in a circle and seated on chairs of stone.

Cunhlat, further along the pine-bordered escarpment road, would, I am sure, have none of such things: a very bustling market-centre full of tall houses and shady gardens, which has clearly thrived on the rich farming country of these grassy foothills. I prefer St Dier whose old houses may well have been rebuilt from the ruins of the priory: the old part lies snug beneath a bluff down which the road winds to cross the fine bridge over a stream hunted by wheeling swifts and waded in by perky yellow wagtails. The priory church, one of the fortified kind with a stout square tower, is early twelfth century; the capitals are primitive but interesting and the stark west facade, much patched, has some lovely purple and rust-red blocks worked into it. Beside it, what remains of the priory now houses, fittingly enough, a Justice of the Peace. Perhaps it is he who keeps the lawn and flower-beds so sparely trim and English. A spot in which one could wile away half a lifetime with the help of a fishing rod and a few companions to drink away the night hours.

Summer visitors might prefer Olliergues on the main valley road, surely the most attractive small town hereabouts, especially when seen 'en panorame', from the steep lane twisting down from Olmet, as an orderly huddle of licheny roofs and dark brown walls, the furthest houses built sheer above the river. The Dove broadens round a shallow bend at this point without noticeably slackening pace. Near here the river once got blocked with boulders which had to be blown apart, upon which the noise made by the sudden rush of water released could be heard (so the tale goes) five miles away. Turenne, the great seventeenth-century general was born here, but only by accident: the carriage that was to take his mother away to some more sophisticated place of accouchement broke a wheel and the departure was — as the French might put it — 'interestingly' delayed.

Courpierre, too, offers something in the way of entertainment and hotels: another place at which I ate very well on occasion. A flourishing town, this, known chiefly for strawberries and other market-produce and for a beautiful transitional church, tucked away in the upper part of the town, containing a fine sculptured Entombment of Christ and some distinctly original capitals. Courpierre is a good example of the small 'bourg' energetic enough to have learnt new ways by which to prosper.

The châteaux in this area are really too numerous to describe them all in detail, but, of the inhabited ones, Martinanches (between St Dier and Cunhlat) Aultéribe and Ravel are all open to visitors and worth the trouble. I came to Martinanches by Ceilloux: the church there was locked but a pleasant-spoken woman opened it to show me the celebrated 'Virgin and Child'. The Lady is calm, blue-eyed, aristocratic, the child's face sharp, intelligent, clear-cut. The statue is simply carved on a plinth draped with a bronze vestment worked with gold thread and decorated with a tumble of flowers. Not a work of art, like the ones at St Gervazy and Marsat, this Virgin has the quality of 'presence' most of these gentle statues display; I have seldom looked at one without being moved. Martinanches lies just off the main road beyond Ceilloux, quite hidden by a thick clump of trees: the secrecy is deliberate for the place was once an armoury used to supply other military strong points nearby, along a series of underground passages. Richelieu had its towers lopped, so that the pleasant fawn walls have a crouching, retired look, like an old warrior somnolent in repose. My guide was very knowledgeable and the interior proved to be interesting. There is one elegant Second-Empire room, some good china of the *Compagnie-des-Indes* period and a most unusual high-backed chair with a small box attached to its carved top in which the ladies of the time kept their tobacco! The castle still has a drawbridge and a moat, its placid water deep green in the reflection of overhanging trees. And behind it is a charming informal garden, an amiable spot in which to browse away an hour after a good lunch.

Many of the castles about here are remarkably secretive, in the sense that they are, whether deliberately or not, hidden away. Mauzun breaks this rule. Its craggy black-stone mass can be seen through odd gaps in the hills for miles around. Now the haunt of

rooks and picnickers, it was for centuries the prison in which the
bishops of Clermont kept naughty priests. Picking one's way
round the briers and tumbled stone of its gutted interior one
wonders how these sad men who had betrayed their faith or
moral trust — or simply offended their bishop — can have
whiled away their time in this grim place, longing for the
animation of Clermont or the company of teaching Jesuits in
Billom. Even more haunted is Fayet, whose immensely tall
crenellated tower has a habit of disappearing just as you have
made up your mind how to approach it. I was still trying to do
so, on foot, when I encountered one of the few really talkative
countrymen of the Auvergne (normally they will give you a civil
"Good day", remark upon the weather and pass about their
business with a nod). This one, wizened and eager, having first
discreetly assured himself that I was English, launched into a
rambling narrative of his doings in the Resistance; which was
probably all highly interesting. Unfortunately his patois was so
thick I could barely grasp the general drift. Finally, I asked
him — "And were you ever injured?" "Ah, yes," he said,
pointing to what appeared to me a very sound left leg: "An
armoured vehicle passed over me here." After which I left him,
still shouting to a neighbouring fisherman, made my way round
the wooded mound that conceals the castle, and found a garden
entrance leading up through gloomy oleanders. It was a still,
thundery afternoon. Nothing stirred. Nor could I hear a sound as
I suddenly came upon the place — huge, shadowy, blank-
windowed, the greater part of it in good repair yet quite
deserted. But the east wing, which must have been extremely
elegant, with elaborately decorated windows of the sixteenth
century, is a mere shell. Was I looking at this place or was it
watching me? Only a canvas chair under the trees betrayed any
sign of human occupation. I turned and went. No local guide
even mentions this place. I do not think I dreamed it.

Codignat could not be more different though also apt to
disappear unless one keeps a stern directional eye upon it. The
castle is (I think) just off the D.44, not far from Néronde on the
main Thiers — Courpierre road. I know it is at the top of a long,
gravelled lane because, as I turned the corner of this lane I met, or
almost met, a hippopotamus (this was before lunching in
Courpierre). The scaly beast stared at me from behind a flimsy

fence and I looked back at it. A young hippo with a dried-up, melancholy air, it was clearly regretting the absence of tropical pools and oozy acres of slime. It should not complain for this is a most beautiful castle in warm, honey-coloured stone, turreted, restored, in immaculate repair, discreetly shaded by stately trees; every bourgeois's dream of a summer home. On rainy northern days I remember it and wonder whether the hippo survived the next winter.

Finally, Aultéribe and Ravel offer an interesting comment on two aspects of the Auvergne, the former reticent to the point of secrecy, adapting to the landscape but using it for concealment; the other bold, assertive, proud of its history and showing a stern front to the world. Even in winter, Aultéribe can barely be seen through its thick screen of trees although it stands only a few yards off the main road from Lezoux to Courpierre (a sign near Lezoux mysteriously says "*Fondation Onslow de Pierre*"). When I arrived in the early afternoon, a quick green lizard, sunning itself on the elegant outside stairway, was the only sign of life. The bluff golden-brown and red-stone building slumbered in the sun, the gravelled courtyard ended abruptly in a cornfield dotted with poppies. What with this and the encroaching trees, which have quite overrun the protective ditch on the roadside, one has the impression of nature waiting to pounce — a year's neglect and the whole place might disappear into a green shade. However, the guide soon appeared. 'Bien aimable' but not unduly well informed, he seemed obsessed with the rivalry between the bureaucracies responsible for the castles. This is now in the charge of the Ministère des Affaires Culturelles. Basically fifteenth century but rebuilt in the nineteenth it originally belonged to one of the La Fayette, a name that recurs in the Livradois and elsewhere. The British Onslow connection came about through marriage with the de Pierre de Bernis family in the early 1800s and it was Mrs Arthur Onslow, a sister of the lady married to the Marquis de Pierre, who took such a strong affection to the castle she chose to live here; and collected most of the handsome furniture, ranging from Louis XIII to Louis XVI, the oriental china and, I assume, some of the unusually fine paintings: they include a portrait of Henri IV by Pourbus, another of Richelieu of the school of Philippe de Champaigne, two excellent Dutch portraits of the Rembrandt school and a peculiarly haunting little picture of the murdered Louis XVII by Vigée le Brun. Oddly enough the place still has a lived-in air. Which is scarcely true of Ravel, much more of an imposing monument to a haughty past, with its garden according to Le Nôtre terminated by a long balustrade. The view across to the 'Chaîne des Volcans' is superb, for the castle is strategically placed on a bluff high above the tiny village of the same name.

Ravel, originally built in the late twelfth century, was for a short period a royal castle: Philippe III, le Hardi, who married Isabel of Aragon in the cathedral of Clermont, took a fancy to it and his son, Philippe le Bel, gave it to his counsellor and friend, Pierre Flotte.

The latter, whose shrewd, enigmatic face — in the portrait at Riom — proclaims the lawyer-statesman, negotiated the canonisation of his master's ancestor, St Louis, in Rome, was ambassador in Germany, and haggled with the rowdy English Plantagenets. We shall meet several ambitious men of his kind in the Auvergne. Another, Jean Doyat, had his ears cropped, his tongue pierced with a hot iron, and was ordered to be publicly whipped, by a Duc de Bourbon for being too loyal to the king's interests. Flotte, however, eventually became the first layman to be created Chancellor of France; but he was killed, still quite young, at the disastrous battle of Tournai.

In the seventeenth century, the castle passed by marriage into the d'Estaing family. Its most distinguished later master was undoubtedly the Admiral Charles Henri d'Estaing, one of the few Frenchmen to beat the English at sea during the wars of the eighteenth century. He found time, during a long career, to refurbish Ravel in the grand eighteenth-century style we see now. But in spite of his continued services to the régime at sea, the Revolution eventually destroyed him. Suspected of being concerned in the attempted flight of the royal family in 1793 he was arraigned by the 'Terror' and sent to the guillotine. His famous last words are found in most French history books: "When", he flung at his judges, "you have lopped the head from my shoulders, send it to the English — they will pay you dearly for it!"

Proud and defiant words. But Ravel, in its creepered and sun-drenched old age, is still a proud place, with a cobbled central courtyard and a single tower rising above several lopped, pepper-pot 'tourelles' like the echo of a dying trumpet-call. The interior — the furniture slightly faded and worn — has an air of grandeur in retirement, of aristocracy in slippered repose. Not a place, one feels, to be taken over by any nouveau-riche banker, however well-meaning. The guide, a local man, is energetically informative and (for once) the guide-book to the 'Châteaux Vivants' does not play several grace-notes too many when it finishes a long description by quoting Villon's ballad "To the Lords of bygone days". Even if you don't understand a word of French, Ravel is worth visiting in summer for the view from the garden terrace.

V

VOLCANIC SPINE AND ISSOIRE

The Auvergne, as I mentioned earlier, is a country of diverse moods. I have travelled across the highlands of the Monts des Domes and the Monts Dore in many weathers and seen all of them. Strange though it may seem, my most vivid memory of these mountains is of a February Sunday, in brilliant sunshine beneath a sky of pure sparrow's-egg blue, tailing off at its furthest distances into wisps of immensely high cloud. Coming down the steep hill into Le Mont Dore itself the snow was piled high on either side, barely leaving room for two cars to pass; people enjoying the sun in their doorways or taking the chance, so dearly looked forward to by country people, of a leisured Sunday gossip, turned to stare at me as if I were a swallow strayed back out of season. The town centre was dead save for a few ladies in high boots on their way to a favourite pâtisserie for the conventional afternoon-visit gift. On the plateaux the fields of snow dazzled, virginal as a new-born world: I saw no animal or bird, the whole landscape glistened, unmoving, in a white silence. From the newly widened road to Murol the blank walls of its enormous castle seemed to stand out almost indecently stark against this luminous background of blue sky and sparkling white. (In contrast, Murol in sunny autumn withdraws into its leafy ambiance like an old pensioner gently sleeping away this mortal coil).

Unlike the Livradois or the Forez, whose tranquility is sylvan, or the Cantal where man has mastered his landscape without quite taming it, this central region, scoured by time and weather, is always savage. Villages like the two Saulzet — the 'hot' and the 'cold' as they are quaintly named — and Nadaillac, on the beautiful minor road from Theix to St Amant-Tallende seem to huddle into what shelter they can find, as if content merely to survive. The grandest road, at whatever time of the year, is probably the one leading over the col de Guéry to le Mont-Dore, the prettiest — but there are so many it would be invidious to choose. The farmers do make a living somehow and there is no longer any vicious poverty, for the population is sparse and the land offers good grazing. In summer there are even fields of rye and other hard grains. And, increasingly, the tourists arrive from mid-June to mid-September in the valley villages beside the lakes which are such a feature of this region.

Aptly enough this is the area richest in splendid churches: where nature failed to provide, God consoled. I would think He still does, for the Auvergnats, though not a demonstrative people, keep their faith. Their quiet piety burgeons, suitably enough, in spring when the miraculous 'Virgins' are carried up to their summer resting places, and in autumn when they are carried down again in processions which give sufficient cause for bishops to visit and for day-long feasting. The principal festivals are at Besse-en-Chandesse, where Our Lady of Vassivières goes up, rather late, on the second of July, and at Orcival on the eve of Ascension. The three great Romanesque churches are those of Orcival, St Nectaire and Issoire: the latter fits conveniently into this section although it lies at the extreme south-eastern edge of these mountains, on its own '*limagne*' where the land is reputedly the most valuable in all the Auvergne. A fourth church, at St Saturnin in the vineyard country due south of Clermont, is also notable; the quiet late-flowering of Romanesque before it soared into Gothic.

St Nectaire became my favourite among these churches not so much for its sculptures and its modest, sweetly proportioned exterior but for the superb setting. The church, free of all encumbrance, is set on a narrow platform of rock so that it seems to ride the air, as much part of the natural beauty of the setting as the wooded hills beyond the gorge below its southern flank or the towering Puy Ferrand which blocks the view to le Mont-Dore towards the south-west. The best approach is by the D. 150 across the high plateau from Aydat. Seen from a bend in this road just beyond the turning to Champeix, the church comes as a complete surprise, airily alone on the rise of Mont Cornadore which it once shared (it must have been a tight fit) with a medieval castle. The village recedes politely from its foot along the hill the visitor must come down. Gybal describes church and situation concisely: "Mont Cornadore," he writes, "covered with grass, is of an emerald clarity. The church, built of a pumiceous tufa, trachite and lava is grey, fawn and red with, occasionally, a hint of rose in it; colours of autumn." The tiles, he adds, have weathered a velvety green while the peaks themselves are autumn coloured: "For in the distance these brown mountains show up as red, of a shade the great clarity of the air translates into rose-colour". Also, most interestingly, he remarks that the surface of this 'acropolis' is convex and that the architect did not succumb to the temptation to flatten it: ". . . he wished the church should blend into the shape of the mound". This is probably why the interior of St Nectaire, though one scarcely notices the fact, has subtle differences of level; while the builder also took advantage of the convexity of his ground to lengthen the apse.

Of the exterior I can only say that it is perfect in its modesty, in only one place clumsily restored, though the modern bell towers (Couthon's mania for destruction again) are admirably fitting. The interior is a gem; unlike those of Issoire or Notre-Dame-du-Port, the roof-line is low so that the capitals can easily be examined, while the subtlety of scale creates an immediate impression of tranquillity, of the near-presence of the Maker. The sculptures themselves repay several visits. One of them tells the story of St Nectaire, a Greek baptised in Rome by St Peter himself, who gave him this name and despatched him to the Auvergne — 'Arvernum' as it was then called. Legend relates that at the moment of his departure from Rome, as he was about to cross the Tiber, St Nectaire recognised the ferryman for the Devil in person. Yet the young man did not hesitate to place himself beside the rower for he had seen an angel of God striding the sky above. This being so, Satan was obliged to land his passenger safely on the other side. Then, at Sutri, Nectaire caught a fever and died. Informed of this by St Austremoine, St Peter travelled into central Italy and brought the young man back to life, a prescient act since the saint, on at last arriving among the Celts, did the same for Bradulus their chief, and so extended Christian prestige among these heathen. They apparently made no objection when he pulled down the Druid temple on the present site and built the first simple church. The capital which illustrates the resurrection of Bradulus is quite delightful, yet highly skilful in its use of space.

Another capital in the choir shows the passage of the Tiber, with a rather boyishly malicious demon glancing up at the angel whose expression, like that of a gravely assured policeman, seems to say: "Now look! let's have no nonsense or you'll be for another Fall". The most extraordinary capital shows a man astride the back of a goat, his right hand grasping its horn, while his mount looks straight into the eyes of a long-muzzled donkey playing on a harp: this I take to be symbolic of an unnatural order of things — Man riding his lust while music, the purest of God's gifts to him, is mocked by 'the Devil's walking parody on all four-footed things'. Most of the other capitals portray Christ's life and Passion. All are charming in their sincerity and directness, concentrated parables in stone: the traces of colour are, I believe, authentic and not part of the nineteenth-century restoration. The treasury at St Nectaire is exceptional, especially the gold-plated bust-reliquary of St Baudime, surely a portrait from life, with short-cropped hair crisped over the brows, aquiline nose, wide-staring eyes and sensitive mouth: a typical Auvergnat of the twelfth century, one might guess, though the sculptor was from the Limousin. On the way out, notice the narthex, or entrance-porch, with its neat triple-bay arcading along the gallery. An essential feature of Auvergnat as it is of Byzantine Romanesque, this example has not been restored since it was built. The Revolutionaries used the church as a gun-powder store, but the local people are said to have hidden St Baudime away until the fury was past.

Below the leafy bluff on which the church stands is the valley of the Couze de Chambon, the 'rushing waters' from which Cornadore takes its name (St Nectaire Bas, the lower village on the main highway, is a tiny spa). A few miles along this valley road, towards Mont Dore, is Murol, one of the holiday villages, and an attractive one for people who like walking and fishing. Its huge castle, once owned by the d'Estaing family of Ravel, is now the property of the local *Commune*. The pine woods beneath it are delightful — ideal for picnics, open to everybody. Chambon itself is another holiday centre, and has a lake on which the bourgeois placidly exercise their copious meals away, on *pédalos*. Above this lake, less eerie than Pavin or Guéry, is the 'Leap of the Virgin', a ledge from which a young girl in danger of losing her virtue jumped and was miraculously saved from injury. Unfortunately, she tried the same feat again, this time to impress her friends, and did not survive the attempt. The village itself has an interesting twelfth-century church and, in the little cemetery across the road, a most curious round building thought to be a funerary chapel. The experts quarrel about this; Gybal thinks its dome-shape may have been modelled on the mosque of Omar in Jerusalem by Templars back from the Crusades.

'Dore' meant waters in old Celtic. One writer remarks that these mountains are nothing but an enormous "castle of waters". Indeed, the name was formerly written 'Monts D'Or, ". . . for the bounty of their waters and pasturage". The river Dore rises on Sancy and once it has joined the Dogne, whose source lies on the nearby Puy de Cascadogne, it becomes the Dordogne, that gracious river which, after finding its way through the precipitous faults between here and the northern hills of the Cantal, flows west through Périgord to join the Garonne. The Puy de Sancy was once much higher than it is now: thousands of years of erosion have reduced it to a mere 6,000 feet and these scourings account for the boulder-littered, ravine-like character of its slopes. In the process of time the valleys, too, have sunk so that La Bourboule, in a hollow once occupied by a lake, is a good 1,000 feet below Sancy. Again, there is a great deal to interest the botanist — the violet *soldanelle* and the delicate rose-coloured *androsace* flourish here, while the Puy Ferrand is noted for its rare plants. The shrines of Le Mont Dore are said to be the most impregnated with silica of any spa in France, and La Bourboule has been irreverently called the 'Queen of Arsenic' because its waters contain so much of this element.

Both Gauls and Romans took the cure here. Since tradition has it that the bath of the Auvergnat of later times consisted of spitting in the air and jumping sideways, I hasten to add that both these spas are now immaculately hygienic. Whatever their habits may have been the local people have profited enormously from their waters. Le Mont-Dore's reputation for being a 'dirty and disgusting village' changed abruptly in the 1830s when it became a fashionable nineteenth-century watering place; its medicinal springs are especially noted for their healthy effect on the vocal cords (not, one would have thought, that the French need much strengthening in this respect). In its early days, the method of cure was bizarre enough. Clad uniformly in trousers and undershirt of white wool with a protecting hood so that one could scarcely tell male from female, everyone crowded into a great shed, divided in the middle by a screen of pine-branches for reasons of sexual modesty. Once the daily ritual was completed, the rich were carried from the exhausting humidity of the springs by porters who waited outside. The poor, apparently, simply ran away and hid in the neighbouring hay-lofts, much to the annoyance of the owners for their perspiration made the fodder rank and stale. Ulcers, hypochondria and rheumatism were the principal ills cured at this time. The brother of Mirabeau, the famous Revolutionary orator, had a house on the hill called 'Le Capucin' (to which there is now a funicular). His hospitality was famous, and several nineteenth-century writers and artists helped to popularise Le Mont-Dore. Now, it is a bustling, rather ugly town and the principal '*establishment*' looks somewhat like a small railway station from the outside. La Bourboule, less crowded in summer, is also known as 'Le Paradis des Enfants' because it has such a wealth and variety of sweetshops, their concoctions — since people come back to these parts every year — presumably free from arsenic. In winter both places are dead, mortuaries of shuttered houses that open only to the 'colonies' of children who come to use the local ski-ing facilities during the school holidays.

An extremely pretty road out of La Bourboule leads up through beech and chestnut woods to the windy, open plateau of the Artense. Before one reaches it a sign indicates 'La Roche Vendaix'; an overgrown knoll, climbed upon by boy-scouts, is all that remains of this once famous fortress, the refuge during the Hundred Years War of one of the most infamous of all soldier-brigands, Aimérigot Le Marché, who plagued the Basse-Auvergne for years. In case anyone should think such people were mere Mexican-style bandits, robbing the odd traveller and making off at high speed, a contemporary chronicler describes one particular haul as follows: 400 cattle, 2,998 sheep, numerous mules loaded with booty and twelve prisoners led away for ransom. No hit-and-run pillagers these! Against such highly organised gangsters the Duc de Berry, busy with his art collections and the acquisition of land, was useless. Eventually, the King found a capable general and Aimérigot was cornered in La Vendaix. Yet he got away and took refuge with a cousin in the castle of Tounemire in the Cantal; who promptly sold him to the King for 7,000 *livres*. Aimérigot is said to have offered Charles VI ten times that sum for his life, but the king's judges told him the Valois family was rich enough. He was hung, drawn and quartered in 1390 and various parts of him decorated the gates of Paris for a while. Grace-note: his widow, doubtless weary of constant travelling as her husband forsook one stronghold the better to ravage the countryside from another, married a banker.

The only market-centre in this area is La Tour d'Auvergne, once the home of the great military family of that name. Of their castle nothing now remains. In the fifteenth-century Madeleine, a daughter of Jean I de la Tour, married Lorenzo de' Medici, the Magnificent, of the ducal bankers of Florence. What an astonishing new world Renaissance Italy must have seemed to the young girl if she had been brought up in this windswept land infested with wolves and brigands. There is nothing to see in La Tour, but St Pardoux nearby has a beautiful church, until the nineteenth century the parochial church of La Tour itself. Originally Romanesque it has been enlarged throughout the centuries; the 'Gothic' side-aisles are, in fact, sixteenth or seventeenth century, and the beautiful gilded altar-piece dates from 1698, when the choir was added to the nave. In this context a strangely sophisticated piece of decoration that scarcely fits the church (let alone the austere temper of people and countryside) it is, nevertheless, a remarkably accomplished work, attributed to local craftsmen. The ironwork of the main doors is also 'classé'.

St Pardoux is amiable, La Tour itself airy and austerely functional: the most interesting village on the plateau is undoubtedly Chastreix, grouped sparsely on its hill around a huge thirteenth-century church. Always known to a few holiday-makers for the wild beauty of its surroundings and the purity of its air, Chastreix has now become the centre for an experiment in social education. Because the landscape is so open and the roads are liable to be blocked at the first heavy fall of snow, the school has for some years been adapted to take in boarders from all the surrounding villages, as well as children of disturbed background. From this developed a winter-sporting

centre designed to teach children how to ski. This idea in turn has
been further developed so that in summer the complex becomes
an international children's centre to which youngsters of fifteen
different nationalities came in 1969 to live together in
community — surely an admirable scheme that might be more
widely copied.

The church, a fine building in what we should call 'Early
English' and the French call the *'Angevin'* style, is famous for its
'Black Virgin', a twelfth-century statue of the Mother and Child
of singular power and nobility; the strength and elegance of the
hands and of the wide, staring almond-shaped eyes are
remarkable. There are a number of these 'black' statues all over
the Auvergne, the most famous being those at Orcival, Mauriac
and Le Puy. The experts quarrel as to why they should be
painted black and I have read no very convincing explanation.
The Marian cult is certainly widespread over the whole region
and no doubt the exceptionally sacred, healing quality of these
images was fostered by the early Christian fathers in order to
drive underground any vestiges of the fertility cults of Gallo-
Roman times. The 'Black Virgins' are seldom beautiful in the
accepted sense and they entirely lack the sweetness of Italian
Renaissance Madonnas; but they do have 'presence', that
curiously haunting quality which makes one turn and look again
as one is about to leave. In this sense they are truly religious for
they compel the visitor to pause and think freshly, perhaps, upon
the significance and inner meaning of the Virgin and Child as
symbols. Birth and the renewal of life were, of course, vital in a
hard mountain country where to have no child meant the
abandonment of land hardly won, while the importance of
purity in woman, both for itself and for its implication as to
rightness of family-descent in an inward-looking, closely knit
community needs no emphasis.

The wealth of this countryside depends entirely on its
abundant water, derived from the winter snowfall which feeds
innumerable natural springs and small streams. Cattle are brought
up here from the Cantal in late spring and the well-to-do *cantalien*
cattle-breeders have, of recent years, been buying up land in the
area, now the principal source of the grey-crusted and very tasty
St Nectaire cheese (the country to the east, around Tauves and St
Sauves' specialises in the *Bleu d'Avergne*). Once, the region was

also famous for goats, sheep and horse-breeding; but the simple fact is that cattle are more profitable. This must always have been a lonely country and its attraction to the visitor lies precisely in its solitude. Should he be in the mood for tall skies, sweeping views of the Cantal mountains to the south-west, and closer ones of the storm-scoured slopes of Sancy, the Puy Ferrand and the Puy Perdrix above Super Besse, the new ski-ing centre, his only company is likely to be the cows (the local *ferrandaises* and the commoner chestnut-coloured Salers breed) an occasional shepherd or fisherman, and the constant murmur of waters. There are innumerable waterfalls about here as the streams hurry across broken, morainic ground in a series of short cuts.

Such a land lays even more claim than usual, in the Auvergne, to be 'haunted'. The plateau of the Cézallier, east of the N.679, was said to be peopled by fairies especially fond of boys whom they drew into their dances and kept for ever.

And there is one — in the true sense — marvellous story centred on Vernols, a village north of Allanche on the main road to St Flour: in the Middle Ages a lord, returning from his pilgrimage to the Holy Land, heard groans as he reached a particularly lonely spot on the plain. Approaching cautiously he found a hermit dying in a cave off the path, apparently bitten by a wolf that was still hovering nearby, waiting to finish the old man off. The lord drew his sword, drove off the beast and said to the injured man — "Have faith in St John, the great saint who can achieve all things. Here! take this relic and kiss it". Then he proffered the hermit a cross of gold in which was inlaid a bone of the saint, brought back from his place of martyrdom. The old man, however, was too far gone; he touched the relic with his lips and expired. The lord glanced at the wolf, growling at a safe distance, awaiting its opportunity to devour the corpse: "Wolf!" he said, "you see this cross? In the name of St John I command you guard it faithfully until I return". Then he continued on his way to Allanche, to the priory of Albantia, and returned the following day with some monks to help bury the corpse. The wolf was still guarding the body, and there, in front of it, was another body, that of a robber who had tried to steal the cross. An oratory was built on this spot and a kind of festival grew up to commemorate the incident. Every year the 'king' of the feast of St John and his companions rode out of Allanche (so-called

because the knight's relic was *la hanche de St Jean*) by the south
gate and galloped to the oratory, where they heard Mass before
riding back to Allanches and re-entering by the north gate.
Every bourgeois then played host to all who craved hospitality.
This fête lasted three days, and on the second day those boys who
had reached the age of working and bearing arms, were received
into manhood. On the third, the people cut a certain field in
order to have 'the grass of St Jean', for its herbs were believed to
cure illnesses. Finally, they danced around a huge stone called 'La
Pierre Grasse' against which women who wished to become 'big'
with child rubbed themselves — truly, a fantastic mixture of
pagan and christian! "Life has diminished", comments Henri
Pourrat — who tells this story — "like the church of Allanches,
which has had two towers lopped."

Allanche, like Condat at the north-eastern edge of the
Cézallier, has become a holiday-centre, while the latter is well-
known as a *lieu de retraite* to which Auvergnat emigrés return to
build houses and live out their retirement. It is a charming place,
built up and down the slopes of the foothills of the Cantal range,
an excellent centre from which to explore the thickly wooded
Gorges de la Rhue as well as the high upland I have just
described.

For the moment, however, let us return to the Monts-Dore
since there is much to see in the volcanic hills north of the two
spa towns.

The road to Clermont from Murol brings one to the Lac
d'Aydat, where the only personality of the Roman era about
whom any knowledge has come down lived in retirement. This
was Sidonius Apollonaris, son-in-law of the Emperor Avitus,
poet-laureate, sometime President of the Senate and a prefect of
Rome. Not an Auvergnat but a Lyonnais, he seems to have been
an amiable, pliant sort of character, devoted to writing poetry
and to comfortable living in the country of his adoption, which
he is on record as having loved dearly — a sort of Gallic
Theocritus. Somehow he also found time to become its bishop;
but his most famous oration was a speech in praise of his brother-
in-law on the occasion of his being elected emperor, for which
the local folk raised a statue to him. These were changeable
times, however. Soon, the emperor was assassinated and the
locals promptly erected a statue to the assassin. Sidonius, one

feels, was not the man to take offence at such expedient proximity or at the slightly suburban air his lake-retreat now has, its tranquil beauty not — as yet — wholly marred by the efflorescence of holiday villas along its wooded slopes.

North-west again, across a deeply folded range of minor volcanic peaks, lies Orcival, site of our second great Romanesque basilica. Such a tiny village, a mere cluster of stone houses, could scarcely warrant a huge church like this, but some evidence of another Druid temple, like that at St Nectaire, may explain the continuity of its religious tradition. The original Christian church was destroyed by Norman raiders, but the 'Black Virgin' was saved and monks from La Chaise-Dieu were called in to re-establish the shrine. They built modestly; but so many people came to worship that more money was found and the present church was begun about the middle of the twelfth century. There is a tale that the master-mason threw his hammer in the air, vowing to build where it landed; which may account for the cramped placing of the basilica right below the hill on the western edge of the hollow. The nearby stream had to be re-routed and part of the hill cut away, hence the absence of any imposing frontal facade. Nevertheless, the church 'grew' even as it was being built, for there are two columns that lack the double arch they were built to support. A contemporary art-historian remarks that Orcival shows the Auvergnat taste for balance, proportion and functional propriety at its best. This may well be true. It is certainly a building of great harmony and integrity, but it takes some getting used to and must be visited on a morning when the light is good. The church is remarkable, also, for having only one storied capital, showing the miser with a rope round his neck, symbolic of the burden of riches on this earth. A common enough theme in the region as a whole, the motif is peculiarly fitting in this austere church whose only *raison d'être* is the Lady it enshrines. She herself, on a pedestal behind a simple altar-block of Lozère stone, has two aspects "au visage grave et dissymétrique", as Craplet puts it — the left side of the face seems to be that of a local country-woman, the right "that of a very great lady, hieratic and royal".

Orcival remains one of the holy places of the Auvergne although the hospital to which sick pilgrims came in great numbers has long since gone. Other lay hotels have replaced it and they offer an equally honest if less austere welcome to the many visitors. But to appreciate the splendid proportions of the church one needs to climb the opposite hill and look down upon it; or take the D.74 towards Vernines and stop for a few moments at a bend in the road from which both village, with its lichened grey roofs, and tall sombre church can be seen cosily *en groupe*.

Up the other hill to the north-west one catches a glimpse of Cordes, built of a hard crystalline granite that reflects rather than absorbs light. No feudal refuge this but a domestic retreat all turrets and lauze-tile roofs, green lawns and neatly clipped evergreen shrubs. Only the one square tower, its crenellation partially disguised by a shallow, tiled 'cap' — like a guardsman in mufti — hints at a more military past. Story-wise we are in Saint-Simon country — that is, in the land of court-gossip at the time of Louis XIV. A rather egregious and pompous courtier, Monsieur de Barbézieux, had married a daughter of the Maréchal d'Allègre, whose country-seat Cordes was. Her husband treated her rather like a child that has to be petted and spoiled, and showed himself complaisant towards her *galanteries* which, unwisely as it turned out, he chose not to take as reflections on his honour. The girl, not unnaturally piqued at such nonchalance, resolved to make him more observant in these matters and unhappily succeeded all too well — her husband became so jealous he took offence at every small compliment and made himself a laughing-stock at court. Finally, he took to declaring himself deceived in public at every conceivable opportunity so that the King — at the urgent request of the d'Allègre family — had to banish the girl to Cordes. After which they packed her off to a convent (possibly to Blesle where, as we shall see, the rule was by no means strict). An odd, bitter, little tale that reflects no credit on anybody.

More scabrous still, but with a curiously gentle dénouement, is that of an earlier d'Allègre, Christophe II, whose life spanned the difficult years of the late sixteenth century — when Henri IV was trying to recreate a kingdom out of the religious turmoil — and the early seventeenth. At first Christophe distinguished himself so much in the wars against the Catholic League that Henri made him governor of Normandy; but he behaved so badly towards the people that he had to be relieved. The first general the King sent to take over, Christophe had placed over a barrel of gunpowder to which was attached a delayed-fuse, the victim being coolly informed that the length of its burning corresponded exactly to his future span, while the second was brutally despatched by M. d'Allègre and his friends with some twenty-five thrusts of dagger and sword. Then he changed sides, was captured, seemingly doomed. Yet he wriggled free once more and took flight to the other bastion owned by the family, at Allègre in the Haute-Loire, not far from Le Puy. "Here", says the chronicler, "it seems the Auvergne returned him to ideas much wiser, pious and even edifying". Adding, however, that it was likely that his wife, Louise de Flageac, whom he married in 1608, had upon this tyrant "a most salutary influence". Possibly. At any rate, she bore him a dozen children. Such a brood might curb anyone's aggressive instincts.

Less fortunate in his amorous career was Yves V d'Allègre, the King's Sénéchal at Le Puy. Badly wounded at the siege of Issoire in 1577 he returned home to recuperate. Already separated from his wife, he was payaing court to another woman who, believing him married, had refused his advances. Still, he eventually seduced her and in revenge she plotted his murder. Promising that she would come to him on a certain night when he should leave an outer door unlocked, the lady arranged for three men disguised as women to enter his chamber. One of them, approaching the bed with outstretched arms as if to embrace him, plucked a dagger from his cloak and stabbed the Sénéchal. He eventually died of thirty-seven separate thrusts!

It seems hardly surprising that the d'Allègre family-line did not survive the eighteenth century — the grand-daughter of Mme. de Barbézieux was the last in direct descent. When I visited Cordes, a charming lady in a housecoat, suddenly appearing from a side-door, apologised to my guide for disturbing her. She was, presumably, Mme Pechaud, the present châtelaine, and visitors may be sure she carries no dagger concealed in duster or pocket. The rooms one may see are unusually gracious, the plaster decoration particularly so. Cordes, whether house or garden, bears eloquent witness to the good taste of its owners, who only bought it in 1965. Passed from hand to hand during the 30s and in the post-war years it had apparently fallen into a shocking state before the Pechauds restored it with the help of the Beaux-Arts. Do not be put off by the massive iron gates of the garden-entrance — they open mysteriously at the bidding of an electric bell in the house itself.

Once across the N.89 at Rochefort-Montagne, we are in the gentler, rolling country of Combrailles from which the volcano-peaks, though frequently seen, are only distant ogres. Let us strike back across the Cheire and over the col de la Ventouse to St Saturnin, eminently worth seeing for its late Romanesque church but also a handsome village (its inhabitants might prefer the term *bourg*, which implies a small township). Certainly the most charming place in this area, in fact, for it has quite retained its late-medieval atmosphere without becoming 'quaint', still less neglected. From the open *place* at its centre we climb steeply along narrow lances towards the castle. In this quarter I did see several empty houses, some time abandoned; but others had already been nicely restored and two were in process of rebuilding. A Giscard d'Estaing lived in the castle which also had connections with the de La Tour and with the de Broglie, on the evidence of inscriptions round the fountain on the rise opposite. Now, it is partly let to an Order of nuns and may not be visited. From this open space the church can at last be seen, the only major one in the Basse-Auvergne to have kept its tower and spire intact. Originally a benedictine priory, it was built in the second half of the twelfth century and one notices, at once, the tall, rather slabwalled sides and the absence of the familiar radiating chapels branching out from the apse. The design is basically 'transitional'.

Personally, I do not find the exterior attractive except for the graceful treatment of the east end and the delicate balance of the arcading on the base which supports the tower. The west end, cramped by lack of space (one literally looks down upon the houses in the lane below) is plain dull, but the interior is both grand and gracious, evidently the object of loving care and attention both now and in the past. This is possibly due to the presence in this upper part of the town of a colony of artists and writers, mostly local people or Clermontois who prefer the quiet of St Saturnin to the clamour of the city. The columns are heavier than those at St Nectaire and there are no storied capitals, another sign of late Cluniac influence. Yet the proportioning is so exact one scarcely misses the spatial extension of the usual ambulatory and apsidal chapels. That St Saturnin, unlike St

Nectaire, Issoire and Orcival, was not a place of pilgrimage may explain this fundamental variation of style; for these features are not merely decorative, they had the practical purpose of allowing a concourse of pilgrims to move steadily past the chapels whose altars contained holy relics; or, if they wished, to kneel at prayer in the chapels themselves without risk of being trodden or jostled by the moving throng.

Outside the church one immediately notices the unselfconscious charm of the little square, a trifle reminiscent, to me, of the Ile St Louis in Paris; and the lovely view down the valley of the Monne towards the twin *bourg* of St Amant-Tallende, a couple of kilometres away — particularly fine in the late afternoon when the declining sun throws bars of sunlight across the trees on the cliff opposite. What was a cemetery is now a little garden and one may sit on the wall, which in turn overlooks someone else's garden on the terrace below, and simply gaze downstream, caught in a verdant silence that would surely have drawn a poem from Andrew Marvell. The little chapel which guards this garden is eleventh century, and dedicated to St Madeleine.

St Amant, on the other hand, quite lacks charm and interest unless one strikes right, upon entering the town, down the very last street overlooking the valley. Here there are some fine houses. And, as the road dips, a humpy, very old bridge across the Monne comes into view: on the left, raised high above the street behind its terraced garden, is the Château de la Tour-Fondue, an excellent example, gargoyled and in full crenellation, of 'Victorian' Gothic. St Saturnin and St Amant remind me of two placid old ladies, their past a trifle dubious though discreetly veiled by time — the one demurely reticent on her hill, the other a mite commercial but presenting a firm face to the world and not without her charms.

Across the main road to Issoire, below the vineyards of Corent (which produce the best Auvergne *rosé*) lies Vic-le-Comte, another old and well preserved town that has recently been awarded the privilege of printing paper for the Banque de France: Clermont actually prints the notes. The stone hereabouts is of a beautiful deep honey-colour and Vic has suffered no ugly restorations. Once a fortified town and the capital of the comté d'Auvergne (as opposed to the Duché, whose capital was

Clermont) its cherished possession is a Sainte-Chapelle, rather finer than the duc de Berry's creation at Riom. The nave is nineteenth-century and the balustrade was added by Catherine de' Médici into whose possession the Comté came while the Auvergne was being absorbed, piecemeal, by the Crown. The windows, though restored, are remarkable of their kind but the Chapelle is full of interesting things and well repays a visit. The church of St Jean, hidden in a tortuous wind of streets, has some good frescoes of the thirteenth and fourteenth centuries. The country to the east of the town is beautifully wooded and well-known for wild flowers. From Vic the D.220 drops us down to Coudes, where the Allier and the Couze de Chambon meet.

St Yvoine, behind the escarpment overhanging the main Issoire road, is not famous for anything. Perhaps it should be for here live two brothers, farmers, to my way of thinking by far the most admirable characters to figure in the film *Le Chagrin et la Pietié*. This four-hour documentary 'epic' on the subject of who resisted during the four-year occupation of France by the Germans, and who did not and why, ran for two weeks to packed houses in Clermont, about which much of its story centres. The elder of the two brothers, a big man for an Auvergnat, was active in the Resistance. Betrayed to the Gestapo by a man of his own village he returned to St Yvoine from the concentration-camp weighing little more than a twelve-year old child. Yet, when asked by the interviewer, "Did you never think of finding out who betrayed you and taking revenge?" he simply shrugged and answered in effect: "I know the man. But what purpose would it serve to unmask him?" If this is not true nobility of character I do not know what is.

So far as one can see, Issoire suffered no violence at the hands of the Germans. But it endured a great deal, and contributed its own share in a past that dwindles into silence about the turn of the seventeenth century. It will be interesting, later, to compare Aurillac, principal town of the Cantal, with Issoire because both, after two centuries or more of anonymity, are now resurgent, full of life and bustle: sharp contrast with say, Riom which has the feel of a dormitory town content to rest upon its past. The little sketch map in *Michelin Guide Vert* betrays instantly that Issoire was once a walled town for its ring-boulevard clearly follows what must have been the line of the walls, the smaller

streets radiating inwards like a series of bent spokes towards the
'place' that is still the site of an open market.

"*Jaunâtre et frotté de maure comme on teint d'ascète*"* observes
Pourrat accurately: for the town houses are of a basically fawny
colour tinged with odd shades of browny-purple and the taller
ones are demurely ascetic. Pourrat goes on to observe, in his
chatty way, that Georges Auric lived here and that Cocteau
visited him. By no means irrevelant, for the town is culturally
'alive' and the people are brisk, helpful and intelligent. I once lost
my spectacles while staying at Valbeleix, up the valley of the
Couze, and trailed despondently into Issoire expecting to wait at
least a week for a new pair. The optician tested my eye-sight and
stood back, inclining his head in approval as French people do
when they have taken one practical step and are ready for the
next. Hopefully, I suggested I might come back in three days'
time. He stared at me for a moment. "The glasses", he remarked
tersely, "will be ready by 11.30." It was then a quarter past nine.
They were, and I am wearing them to this day.

The city existed in Charlemagne's time, when it was famous
for learning: the Emperor built a bridge across the Allier when
he passed through on his way south and stayed awhile to visit the
schools. St Austremoine had already been here in the third
century and founded the church. Long afterwards in 1540,
arrived a much humbler person, a German monk of the Calvinist
faith who dared to preach in the town and made some converts.
Out of which sprang all the trouble of the next fifty years. The
German monk soon demanded the right to preach in the church
of St Austremoine but was chased out by the verger. However,
one of the citizens, Jean Brugière, refused to deny his belief when
summoned to do so and was burnt at the stake. Not unnaturally,
this martyrdom made further converts and Issoire became known
throughout France as "a little Geneva". The struggle for power
fluctuated between Protestant and Catholic factions until, in
1575, the redoubtable Merle — whom we have already
encountered at Ambert — arrived before the city. Needless to say
he took it and proceeded to demolish its Catholic heritage by
knocking down the towers of the basilica. According to legend
he also ordered one of the pillars of the nave to be sawn through,

*"Yellowy and touched with purple like the complexion of an ascetic".

hoping the building would fall down; but it did not. In lighter humour Merle had some of the leading Catholic citizens paraded through the place on donkey-back, while others were pelted with rotten vegetables. Then he went off to assault any other town foolish enough to resist him, leaving the Protestant faction in command.

This, inevitably, brought down a royal army under the King's brother, the Duc d'Alençon, who brutally bombarded Issoire but failed to take it until an unfortunate misunderstanding on the part of the defending citizens let in his troops during a truce. The duke's soldiers behaved even worse than the guerrilla-leader, Merle; they virtually rased the town, which accounts for the absence of any medieval houses. Happily (perhaps because it stands well clear of the surrounding buildings and so could not be destroyed by fire) the church escaped serious damage. It is a fine building and one can appreciate it all the better for being able to stand back and look at it from the open ground behind the apse. Here, and at Brioude, which comes into the next chapter, the skilful way in which the local architects built up their rounded masses, lightening each stage with mosaic or other decoration and with subtle variations in the colour of their stone, can be seen to superb effect. To northern Europeans more accustomed to the soar and splendour, the sheer complexity of Gothic I can only say: be patient, these buildings grow on you. Above all they adapt most admirably into their surroundings, as we shall see at Lavaudieu.

The interior at Issoire has been most abominably painted. Ruined, some might say. I do not agree although I was appalled by the dull sour greens and lustreless reds when first I walked into this church. In the end, one can ignore the abject colouring and I hardly need to beg the reader to concentrate on the sculptured capitals, whose treatment is more sophisticated than that at St Nectaire. This, in itself, would not necessarily recommend them if they were not also truly and movingly 'humanist' in the original not the Renaissance sense of that word. Although their primary purpose was to teach through illustration these sculptors never lost touch with the world they lived in; the Roman soldiers, chain-mailed, uncomfortably asleep on the hard ground of Gethsemane are drawn from life — there is no attempt to abstract, still less to prettify or elaborate in order to emphasise the

skill of the artist himself. Yet these sculptors were extremely
skilled in their use of confined space: every detail leads on the
eye, without effort, to the next, while the volute and foliage
decoration at the angles of the capitals are not merely decorative,
they also perform a structural role in helping to support the
arches. Detailed description would be superfluous; but the
portrayals of the Last Supper and of Christ rising from the Tomb
are marvellous examples of what I have been trying to say.

Issoire is not an immediately attractive place yet it improves
upon acquaintance (the aluminium and light-engineering
factories that contribute to its prosperity are all on the outskirts).
The hotels are unpretentious but good, and one eats well almost
anywhere in the town.

Within easy motoring distance there is a great deal of interest.
To the west, up the winding valley of the Couze and through the
oddly named 'gorges du Courgoul', Besse-en-Chandesse makes a
pleasant luncheon-stop. The gorges themselves, though sombre
on an overcast day because so steep-sided and thickly wooded
until one reaches Valbeleix, are delightful in good weather. St
Floret, where the Germans massacred a handful of citizens after
the local maquis had fired on one of their vehicles, has some
interesting frescoes in its ruined castle and others in a chapel
perched on the bluff to the south. If you are feeling venturesome,
an abrupt turn left in Saurier offers a precipitous climb to the
high plateau, haunt of buazzards, kestrels and placidly chewing
cattle, from which there are sweeping views of the Livradois,
blue-back and shadowy to the east, and of the bare peaks of the
Monts-Dore off right. This road brings you back via Mayrand
and Compains, past the windy Lac de Moneineyre, along a
very high road, some 3,800 feet up, to Besse. This is singularly
wild country but the villages — Compains especially — are
quite civilised and beginning to cultivate the passing traveller.

Besse itself is so immediately charming that people fairly flock
to it all summer. Turreted, steeply set and noticeably well-built in
the fifteenth- and sixteenth-century style, it wears a proud
baronial air. Marguerite de Valois — la Reine Margot about
whom not only Dumas told tall stories — stayed briefly in a
particularly coquette house in the town-centre. One can only hope
its summer popularity will not tarnish this sobre charm. The
church, a trifle over-restored, houses in winter the celebrated

'Black Virgin' of Vassivières who had herself taken up to that windy hamlet on the horns of a cow, one season the Bessois neglected to carry her there. Now immaculate, the church lay in ruins after the Revolution, when the *enragés* demolished its bell-tower as well as the one over the crossing. The capitals, described by Foeillon as *"les plus farouches et peut-être les plus savants de l'Auvergne"* do in fact reflect a pagan and Old Testament strain less common elsewhere though often present in the form of cruel-beaked griffons, a minotaur-like beast and the Atlas-figure carrying the weight of the arch upon his stone shoulders.

This must, one feels, have been a remote, pagan country until very recent times. Storms boil up with startling suddenness in high summer, the clouds seeming to gather into grey writhing spirals visibly curling and uncurling in the swift upward currents of air, only to quieten and disappear, as if by some airy magic, should the thunder not break. Lac Pavin, cobalt-blue and reputedly over 1,000 feet deep in its circular volcanic crater, is positively sinister. No amount of *pédalos* and eager, chattering visitors will persuade me some strange monster does not lurk in these depths (there are, in fact, whirlpools it is dangerous to approach). Only in 1726 did the locals dare to go out in a boat to plumb it and they failed to touch bottom. Stones thrown into it were said to produce cracks of thunder and mysterious aerial disturbances, while there is the usual legend of a city beneath its ominously still waters.

From Besse one may return to Issoire by another high road across the escarpment above the Couze valley, by the grottes de Jonas where the bones of prehistoric animals have been found; past St Diery which has a massive and very private castle with a Romanesque chapel attached, somewhat difficult of access (I should know as I fell off a wall trying to find a way into it); and Montaigut-le-Blanc, oddly named since it is a rich golden-brown, where the ruined castle is being patiently restored by a Clermont architect planning to live in it. One hopes he does not meet the sad end of the Templars who once defied kings from its walls. Personally, I would prefer the lovely late medieval house opposite the church, almost Moorish within the shady seclusion of a courtyard and wrought-iron gates.

The main road south to Brioude accompanies the Allier — at a respectful distance — across the richly fertile plains. Off right, just before St Germain-Lembron, through Chalus which has its own castle, lies Villeneuve-Lembrun, a curiously derelict village for so prosperous a countryside; Mareugheol immediately below on the plain tells the same tale of emigration, of whole families departed, leaving the farmers who remain a richer patrimony — or so it would seem from the prevalence of the latest models of tractor. The short detour to Villeneuve is worth while in order to see the château, its huge, round, fawn towers and shiny blue tiles in marked contrast to the crumbling brown stone of the neighbouring houses. Here lived, in the relatively tranquil early years of the sixteenth century, Rigaud d'Aureille, High Chamberlain to four kings; in effect a distinguished civil servant who accompanied Charles VIII to Naples on his grand campaigns, was sent on a mission to the Knights of St John at Rhodes and commissioned to restored order to this region once the soldier-brigands like Aimérigot and Bernard Garlan, 'the Wicked Hunchback', had been suppressed. From his portrait in the castle courtyard he looks a shrewd, far-seeing man, leaning on his long cane-of-office, soberly dressed in a long knee-length black cloak with the voluminous sleeves of the period. Evidently a fine organiser, he was put in charge of receiving the king's troops, back from Italy in 1508 — a vital task considering the depredations such soldiers, disbanded but unpaid, had committed during the Hundred Years War.

Yet, ironically enough, his castle — restored in the seventeenth-century manner by another court-servant — is best known for the weird and grotesque frescoes adorning the walls of its ground-floor gallery which overlooks the handsome inner court. These represent, as a form of sublimation perhaps, his contemporary reputation as a deceived husband; the most startling painting shows a savage and emaciated creature, half-wolf, half-monster, snarling viciously. This represents the beast that devours only women faithful to their marriage vows. Hence its half-starved condition. The other beast is grossly over-fed and sinisterly complacent, for it feeds upon those women who deceive their husbands. A curiously surrealist reflection upon the psychology of an otherwise admirable and successful man: one wonders whether he was not deliberately cocking a visual snook at the court-gossips of his time.

This castle, now owned by the State, was being restored in

1972 and the interior was not very interesting. The site is beautiful however, and the church across the village-green, with the Aureille arms over its main door, merits a glance.

To the east of the main road rise the foothills of the Livradois, marked by a succession of conical hills, known locally as *buttes*, rather like those of central Italy. Two of them once bore famous castles: that of Nonette was the favourite refuge, when Riom became unsafe, of Jean de Bourbon, duc de Berry. So precipitous is the hill that the place must have been virtually untakeable; from its ruined but still massive walls once looked a much fiercer warrior, Thomas de la Marche — bastard son of the Valois — who was given the job of chasing Robert Knollys, a persistently rapacious British adventurer, from the Basse-Auvergne. This he did, but after the peace of Bretigny the court influence of the Bourbons enabled Jean to prise it from him. Not unnaturally offended, Thomas took to brigandage on the grand scale, reclaimed Nonette and held Riom to ransom, only to die, suddenly and mysteriously, a year or so later. The cunning duke then made of Nonette his prize possession, filling it with precious works of art. Yet nothing this man did was to any good purpose: to pay for his art-treasures he levied high taxes on the burgesses of St Flour and ill-treated them when they could not pay, while his officers were so unpopular in Aurillac they had only to appear on the streets for a riot to begin.

The views are splendid on all sides — a site not to be missed. Usson, perched on a very similar hill-top a few miles away, can clearly be seen from Nonette. On the way there spare a moment for the church at Mailhat, very old, probably eleventh-century, and built of the tawny local stone; it has some remarkable primitive carvings. Notice the woman with the serpent at her breast on the south portal and the decorative work along the cornices. The interior is high, grand, almost empty but for a fine wooden Christ with his head partly eaten away by woodworm. What a pity the Ministry of Fine Arts does not take this church in hand, for it is in a sad state of disrepair.

The castle at Usson may be seen in its pristine flfteenth-century state, all airy towers and with a massive square *donjon* in an old painting at the château of Parentignat, nearer Issoire; this picture makes it so resemble those delightful castles high above flowery meadows depicted in the duc de Berry's illuminated missal, *Les*

Tres Riches Heures that one wonders whether it might not have been one of the painter's models. To Usson came Margeurite de Valois, after she had separated from her husband and had been expelled by him from Carlat, above Aurillac. This intelligent, volatile woman lived for some twenty years here, holding rustic court, reading, changing — if the stories are true — lovers from time to time. For political reasons her warder, the Marquis de Canillac, kept her under strict watch and, acting on instructions from the Court, had her young favourite, the Chevalier d'Aubiac, beheaded. Surprisingly Marguerite rewarded him with a house in Paris worth a great deal in rents and loaded his wife with jewels: both the Canillacs then went off to Paris to lord it at Court. Unknown to them, however, the Queen had already sent on a messenger to the capital, with advice to her lawyer not to grant the house and to reclaim the jewels. Red with shame the Canillacs soon returned to Usson, and one can imagine Marguerite's ladies giggling discreetly behind their fans at the unjewelled marquise.

It can scarcely be true that the Queen kept d'Aubiac's head preserved in a travelling bag, which she carried about with her. Certainly she occupied herself with good works among the country people — perhaps riding side-saddle on the camel another story credits her with. I would like to believe this one for, from all accounts, Marguerite was an eccentric but charming lady. Who could begrudge the bereft Queen her amours in this high, lonely place so remote from the Renaissance culture she loved?

Unfortunately, very little remains of the fabulous castle on its *butte* above the tiny village. Again, the views are grand — some consolation at least, for Margot and her ladies. I have always fancied a house at Usson yet there are, sadly, a number of dilapidated ones.

After St Germain-Lembron — a pleasant town once off the busy main street — the road climbs steadily to the plateau. Beyond Mauriat, though historically speaking still in the Auvergne, we enter the province of the Haute-Loire and a rather different kind of landscape.

VI

THE LIVRADOIS AND BRIOUDE

Auzon was one of the 'Thirteen Fine Towns' of the Auvergne, compact fortified 'cities' in the medieval sense, whose burgesses strove to encourage trade — for it was only by trading such towns might grow — and to discourage rapacious barons by whom no-one profited except themselves. Auzon, situated on an eastern spur of the Haut Livradois, is a gem. No lover of the picturesque should miss it. It would be quite easy to do so because, from the modern suburb a mile or so east of the bridge across the Allier, it can barely be seen. One may drive a car up but it is better to walk the steep lane overhanging the stream, past the first tiny cottages quite literally built into the hill. This brings one into what passes for a main street which, broadening to the right, into a narrow square largely occupied by the church, apparently terminates in a fine medieval gateway that must at one time have been the entrance to the central stronghold. To describe Auzon as beautiful would be inaccurate in the context of the Auvergne: Besse, St Flour (on a larger scale) or Blesle are more immediately attractive. What strikes one is the completeness, the well-nigh ridiculous self-sufficiency of the place. How, one wonders, could people have survived long winters in such a tiny, close-knit enceinte without murdering each other? What did they find to do when the day's work was done?

I brought here a north-country friend unused to such places. He swung his camera, paused and shrugged: "It's just too private," he said, "and sort of eerie".

The town's origins are obscure. When the '*Seigneurs*' died off, Auzon passed to the Montmorin, a familiar name in the Livradois, and then to the family of Polignac — powerful, arrogant even to claiming descent from the Roman aristocracy — whom we shall meet nearer Le Puy. Once a fortress of considerable importance Auzon now deserves to be famous for its church, which is unique. For one thing it is built on a narrow platform of rock, presumably to stop it sliding downhill. This necessitates a double flight of steps leading up to the entrance porch, which is supported by three arches. Carved into the capitals of these arches are some fascinating early Romanesque sculptures — unfortunately rather weathered — the most unusual of which portrays Daniel in the lions' den, his hands held to his breast as if in horror at the strange, mythical creatures around him. The best carving, relatively well preserved, is of the Nativity. Joseph, leaning across the Virgin, places one hand tenderly over hers while his long bearded face, hugely expressive yet enigmatically so, draws the viewer into his mind like a magnet. Just *what* is he thinking? To me this portrait is the reverse of naïve, if this quality be taken to mean innocent of complexity. The rest of the exterior is pleasantly functional, very fitting in this ambiance.

The interior, however, contains a wealth of beautiful things. The nave, thought to date from the second quarter of the twelfth century, is — again — simple and massive, the huge double arches framing the gentler harmony of the apse. But it is the marvellous 'Crucifixion' on the far wall that at once draws the eye; there is no more beautiful portrayal of Christ in the Auvergne, and few elsewhere that I know of. A little longer than life-size, draped in a cloth knotted about the middle, the figure has a marvellous simplicity. The power of expression is concentrated, as it should be, in the face. Long, aquiline, the eyes cast downward in a sort of modesty of pain, the sensitive mouth firmly closed yet free of grimace, the exquisitely stylised hair falling in three plaits to either shoulder. A work of art whose 'presence' follows the visitor about the church. In contrast, the Virgin, extremely late Gothic, is perhaps too affectingly sweet — the artist seems to be calling your attention to his skill. Yet the face is truly affecting in its calm refinement; and children do, as this small boy does, lift their eyes in puzzlement and place two fingers to their lips. The other statue, of St Peter, and obviously by the same artist (the high sweeping forehead as well as the treatment of the drapes indicate this) is also very fine in its way. Finally — one had almost said in light relief — there is St

Verny, or St Werner, a young man of Alsace who was the victim of a ritual murder by the Jews in the thirteenth century. (Bernard Craplet traces his cult from Alsace down through Burgundy into the Auvergne where it became popular in the seventeenth century). This figure, probably of Burgundian origin, can only be described as quaint in its homely short-squareness, a quality emphasised by the curious hat, like an inverted bell plonked on a sombrero-style brim. St Verny's parents were vintners, to which the long pruning knife in his right hand and the little barrel at his feet bear witness. A canonical oddity and most unexpected in this church, although one occasionally meets him elsewhere in less charming guise.

There is a good deal else to see: a scrolled pulpit that no-one seems to have fully deciphered, some striking frescoes decently restored and the usual good ironwork, especially on the communion-screen. The church is thought to have been established by monks from La Chaise-Dieu, which may partly account for its riches. One other fascinating object, lost to Auzon, a little box sculptured in whale-bone, is now divided between the British Museum and the Bargello in Florence: it came, the little guide book says, ". . . from far-off Northumbria (England) and was doubtless brought by a pilgrim on his way to St Julian of Brioude". I trust he found good board and lodging in Auzon.

From here a good road, sweeping up into the hills of the Haut-Livradois, offers, unexpectedly, the only complete view of the medieval city stretched precariously alongs its bluff. Soon we are in lonely country indeed: in the whole triangle of roads, marked at its corners by Brioude, La Chaise-Dieu and St Paulieu, there is scarcely a village with more than 200 inhabitants. There are linguistic grounds for believing this now richly forested region was once settled by wanderers from the maritime city of Phocaea on the Ionian coast of ancient Greece. The word Livradois may derive from the Greek *libethron*; while Pourrat, noting the Hellenic ring of such village-names as Dame ('Damas') and Askalon, above Ambert, claims also that the people's feast-day custom of hanging out standards and bunting from the houses, as well as their talent for making canvas-cloth, possibly springs from their sea-going past. However this may be, a countryside once desperately cleared by a too-numerous peasantry in order to grow crops for food has now reverted to its more natural and profitable state of upland pasture and forest. In the nineteenth century, in the autumn, sawyers, each carrying two pairs of sabots and a double-sack closed at both ends but opening in the centre, used to emigrate from villages like Fournols to Belgium, returning to plant in spring and to gather in the summer harvest. Now, the piles of sawn wood on the outskirts of many villages advertise the wisdom of afforestation by the departmental authorities. One result, for the casual traveller, is a magnificently unspoiled mountain landscape no longer marred by the grinding poverty of the eighteenth and early nineteenth centuries.

Half-way to La Chaise-Dieu is Champagnac-le-Vieux, a pleasant village solidly built of houses whose inhabitants have made of it a small holiday-centre; they have even constructed a swimming-pool in order to keep the children happy.

The people of the Haut Livradois are shy but courteous, reminding one a little of the Scots Highlanders in their proud reserve. The wise traveller, before going on to La Chaise-Dieu, will branch left up the wild gorges of St Sauveur and turn left again to Novacelles, so pretty and secluded in its steep-sided arboreal hollow, and encircled by a trout-stream upon whose further bank is a tiny cemetery distinguished by one curious and elegant 'Romantic' monument. The modern tower of the little church — very recently restored — scarcely prepares one for the rustic Romanesque of its interior or the fine frescoes now revealed beneath the plaster. Romanesque in style though probably painted later. The 'Christ in Majesty' is excellent. Such finds help to punctuate the day's travelling; but this deeply folded landscape, rich in hurrying streams that invite one to explore their banks on foot, and in grand views unexpectedly opening out — when the trees fall away — to reveal ridge upon forested ridge as far as the eye can see, is eminently worthwhile in itself.

For those who enjoy looking around churches, that of St Sauveur, across the bridge in the valley below the village itself — which has two excellent hotels — contains a moving little 'Crucifixion' on a gold-work cross in the chancel; St Bonnet-le-Chastel has a handsome fifteenth-century exterior and St Geneste a quaint 'Black Virgin' who stares inperiously from a coquettish blue and gold altar, quite ignoring two angels bowing obsequiously at her feet. Back on the main road, Marsac has a famous Chapel of the Penitents: one has to pay to enter but the guide is sternly but entertainingly informative on this rather masochistic Counter-Reformation cult. From Marsac, across more open rolling country — the southern edge of the Auvergnat Forez — lies Viverols 'la Romantique': a delightful village with the dignified air of having a past which it is unconcerned to reveal to the visitor unless he inquires closely.

Here lived one Hector Granet *greffier de la paix* — presumably Clerk of the Court at Ambert or Arlanc. Anyway, a man of most eccentric tastes for a lawyer. He owned one of these fine houses, tastefully decorated in First-Empire style, full of documents and of cats to chase away the mice that nibbled them; also a little museum with a round tower where he conserved the body of his father in spirits of alcohol. And, if this were not odd enough, he contrived in the basement of his funeral chapel an arrangement by which, on his striking three times the base of the coffer containing his pickled parent, the corpse jerked up like a marionette and appeared at the window of the tower! I explored the neighbouring cemetery to find some trace of the bizarre lawyer, but failed. The ruined castle above the village is worth the short climb — a fine romantic ruin whose grassy tiltyard is now the playground of children.

Nothing so grotesque, one feels, could happen at La Chaise-Dieu; at 3,000 feet, with clear views all round, the 'Seat of God' indeed. Yet it wears the sad, desolate air of piety abandoned. This was the greatest abbey of the Auvergne, founded in the eleventh century by St Robert, one of the soldier-knights who kept the peace and guarded the relics of St Julian at Brioude. In his time there were 300 monks, while three castles and fifteen churches formed part of the abbey's domain. The church we see, which is fourteenth century, was built by a former monk who had become Pope Clement VI. There is no church in this region that can match it for sombre grandeur for it is built high and wide in the style of the southern basilicas. One has to people this place with one's imagination but I always left it with a curious feeling of relief; whether because it is so empty now — a vast ecclesiastical museum — or because the Romanesque churches are so much more sympathetic, I do not know. Somehow, the grim fresco on the north side of the choir epitomises the place: its three panels depict typical figures of noblemen, bourgeois and artisan of the time; but the painting is no mere commemoration of an ordered society at ease with itself and obedient to the will of God. For each man or woman has an attendant shadow, skeletal and beckoning, eternal reminder of the oblivion to come. This 'Danse Macabre' seems to foreshadow the wrath which fell upon La Chaise-Dieu in the high summer of 1562, when a Huguenot army under the sadistically efficient Baron des Ardrets besieged the abbey. The monks had already packed 'La Tour Clementine', built for just such an eventuality, with precious relics, documents and provisions. They survived; but the great abbey township was ruthlessly sacked and pillaged.

From this it never really recovered though, ironically enough, when the royal House soon afterwards took what remained under its charge, a bastard son of the Valois Henri II became its first abbot; he had been one of the assassins of the Protestant leader, Coligny, killed during the Massacre of St Bartholemew's Day.

The most sympathetic personality connected with the place is Jean Soanen, Jansenist Bishop of Senez, born at Riom in 1647, the son — inevitably — of a lawyer. The intrigues and controversies that led to his exile are irrelevant to this book. But, at the age of 80, exiled he was to this high, cold place, following a 'Grand Council' at Lyon, which found his opinions and high conviction too obdurate to bear. They brought him here, across the mountains from Lyon, in a carriage in midwinter. When at last he arrived he was so cold that servants had to carry him, stiff as a board, to his lodging. Yet the austere man asked for the tapestry covering one wall of his room to be removed. The monks then pointed out to him that the tapestry was no mere decoration, for it covered various cracks and holes in the wall that would otherwise let in draughts. Reluctantly, he gave in. Jean Soanen survived here thirteen years and so great was his reputation for probity that many people made the terrible journey to see him. The monastery had sunk so low at this time there were only thirty-six monks left, many of them of the same austere Jansenist belief. Perhaps this was why the authorities sent him to La Chaise-Dieu. At least he could make few converts. From his portrait in the museum at Riom he looks a charming man; and in his prime he was a famous preacher.

'La Tour Clementine' still stands and the magnificent cloister is being restored. Inside the church, the oak choir stalls, the sixteenth-century tapestries and the late Gothic screen are all exceptionally fine. The little town, which the tourist-trade has helped to revive, is pleasant enough though one notices the preponderance of old people, another sad reminder of glory departed.

Allègre, some thirty kilometres down the secondary road to Le Puy, has the same reserved, self-contained air of the hill-top town. Even higher than La Chaise-Dieu, it is built along the shallow curve of an amphitheatrical hill at the northern end of which stand two round towers joined by a crenellated battlement. From the distance these look like the pillars of a Roman temple: they are, in fact, all that remains of the Château d'Allègre, original seat of the family whose disastrous amours we encountered at Cordes. Such towering and isolated splendour, added to the stories, invites to *son et lumière*. So far there is only *lumière* but the town itself makes an interesting walk. It has a less disconsolate air than La Chaise-Dieu, thanks no doubt to the saw-mills by the station which provide local employment.

Before going down into the Velay, however, there is a great deal of interest — quite apart from the town itself and its superb church — around Brioude. A good road back to the narrow plateau which carries the main highway from Brioude to Le Puy is the D. 22, just below La Chaise-Dieu. This follows the path of the Senouire, one of my favourite rivers: I once spent half-an-hour precariously balanced on large flat stones tugging an assortment of white, pink and blue-striped rocks from its bed. Paulhaguet need not detain the visitor though it would make a good centre for anyone wishing to browse through these high, wooded hills and valleys where the silences are so deep the splash of a stream over a waterfall or the sudden chatter of jay or magpie seems indecently loud. Above Paulhaguet the Senouire makes a sharp turn past Domeyrat (which has a huge ruined castle and a tiny early Romanesque church built of almost uncarvably hard granite) into the valley where stands Lavaudieu.

This hamlet — for it is little more now — has none of the eeriness of Auzon; its chief quality is repose. Clasped shyly into a hollow of the escarpment that carries the main road it is, also, scarcely visible from its own private valley, so nearly do the

browny-black walls blend into the landscape. A wide main street
and a huddle of ancient houses dropping to the little bridge over
the Senouire are all the lay part of it; the rest comprises the
abbey-buildings and the late eleventh-century church. The
frescoes the latter contains, especially the Apotheosis of the
Virgin, the graceful angel over the west door, and the story of St
Ursula, are well-preserved in view of the dampness of the
church. The treatment of the robes in these paintings seems to
indicate a Byzantine influence. The cloister, entered through an
arched doorway in the adjoining building, is one of the finest I
have seen anywhere in France. The only one intact in the
Auvergne, and cunningly restored, its charm lies in the austere
delicacy of its decoration and in the sense it affords of absolute
withdrawal, of having remained not only architecturally but
spiritually intact. As if to emphasise this, a beautiful fresco of the
Virgin in Majesty has been uncovered in the adjoining chapter-
house. Beyond the cloister, a charming garden looks over the
Senouire to the fields and to the farm-road, leading up from the
old bridge, which winds into the hills, here as gently enfolding as
those of La-Chaise Dieu are grand and remote.

Our modern world, in which the turbulence of the well-
intentioned is almost as remarkable as that of the evilminded,
tends to question the discipline as well as the retirement of the
monastic ideal. It may be right so far as the twentieth century is
concerned. But during the early Middle Ages when Lavaudieu
flourished, such abbeys were the only possible refuge from the
violence of Nature and from the brute-intolerance of one man
for another. Order there was not, in any human or universal
sense: it had to be created painfully and with great patience, in
the relative calm of these quiet places, by men who had the
spiritual experience of a Divine Order.

Aptly enough, there are no stories extant concerning
Lavaudieu. About the more extrovert St Julien de Brioude there
are plenty. The most gruesome is that of a deacon of this church
who stole a sheep and denied the fact to the shepherds who came
to reclaim it, saying arrogantly — "St Julien does not eat
mutton". Shortly afterwards he was taken with a fever so bad he
felt himself being consumed, inwardly, to a cinder. So he begged
to have water thrown over him to cool his parched body: "And
soon such a great cloud of smoke and such a horrible smell

enveloped him that all around fled". Could it have been the odour of burning roast mutton?

More pleasantly and with a happier ending, there is the tale of St Bergette, a medieval shepherdess who felt such devotion towards St Julien that the saint used to enable her to pass across the river in miraculous fashion in order to worship at his tomb in the great basilica. One day, as she approached the river, she stumbled upon some English soldiers hiding in the reed-beds. They allowed her to pass but only on condition she swore not to reveal their presence to the townspeople. Feeling bound to keep her oath she said nothing to anybody; but once in the town she turned her face to the wall and cried out — "Stones! stones! I tell you the enemy is by the river". Naturally, the citizens could not help overhearing. What the English felt about this nice distinction between piety and patriotism is not recorded.

St Julien himself was a Christian legionary who fled to Brioude from the Rhone valley to escape persecution there, only to be martyred in the town. There is a well, still to be seen in a private garden near the church, into which the Roman soldiers threw his head: if you look down into it (the story goes) you will see the stones tinted red with the martyr's blood. However that may be, a famous shrine was built over the spot where he was beheaded. The first church was destroyed by Normans, raiding up the Allier, early in the tenth century. The magnificent narthex, or outer porch, we see now was constructed towards the end of the eleventh century and the church was completed during the twelfth. It is a superb building though quite different, in proportion as in feeling, from the Romanesque basilicas further north. It can be regarded, in fact, as midway in style between those churches and Notre Dame du Puy; and like the latter it was an important 'stage' for pilgrims making their way to the shrine of St James of Compostella in North-West Spain — hence the soldier-monks, usually of noble birth, who protected it. This Order existed until the Revolution.

Some art-historians consider that St Julien suffers from being — as we should term it — 'transitional'. The central apse has ogival vaulting, while the decoration at the east end is unusually luxuriant and free in style. Personally, I do not find this ebullience disturbing and always returned to the church with pleasure. The interior is grand and high and the sculptures on the capitals, particularly those on the pillars of the nave, repay careful examination. One can, indeed, perceive the development of Auvergnat sculpture as one passes from narthex to abulatory where, as Craplet remarks, that early Gothic 'humanism' which reaches its peak in the great Romanesque cathedrals of Burgundy is easily remarked. The stone, of the familiar deep-honey colour picked out in darker browns, blue-black and russet-red, is beautiful throughout; while modern restoration has uncovered excellent frescoes, notably in the chapel dedicated to St Michel; here there are genre as well as religious scenes, including one of masons, trowel in hand, about their business.

Perhaps the most riveting feature of the interior, however, is the so-called 'leprous Christ' on the south wall, above the curious and (I believe), unique rendering of the Virgin in Childbirth. This fifteenth-century 'Crucifixion', said to have been carved by a leper from a nearby hospital, is a truly horrifying exercise in realism — as if, in addition to the known sufferings of Christ, had been added those of a terrible disease of the blood. Whether the artist intended that effect or not, the statue, in its dire evocation of sheer human pain, is a most haunting expressionist vision that I cannot possibly forget. The handsome gilded '*Vierge à l'Oiseau*' on the other side of the nave will remind the visitor of the one at Riom: some judges think it superior and it is certainly less studiedly refined. Recent excavations have discovered Roman flooring beneath the tiles in the body of the church, and one has the impression that the people here are rightly proud of their shrine and its long 'pilgrim' heritage. The west end and south facade are unfortunately hemmed in by the surrounding houses. But, as at Issoire, a *place du marché* behind the apsidal chapels enables one to admire their handsome proportions, the sturdy barlong which balances the rounded masses below, and the dainty yellow and green-tiled spire over the arcaded tower.

Between the two World Wars, Brioude and its *arrondissement* lost over 14,000 people through emigration to Clermont, Paris and other urban centres for, although the birth-rate was relatively low, this countryside simply could not support a large population. Now it is a flourishing, expanding township, well-built though of no outstanding architectural interest, rather labyrinthine, amiably preoccupied with its own affairs. I always find it one of the most cheerful places in the Auvergne and its

Orcival; Romanesque church

Château de Cordes near Orcival

St Austremoine at Issoire—a storied capital

St Austremoine at Issoire, twelfth-century

St Yvoine from the Ribeyre

The Black Virgin of Vassivière borne through Besse

Auzon; Romanesque church porch

La Chaise-Dieu; Abbey church, fourteenth century

Old Brioude from the Allier

Château de Chavagnac-Lafayette

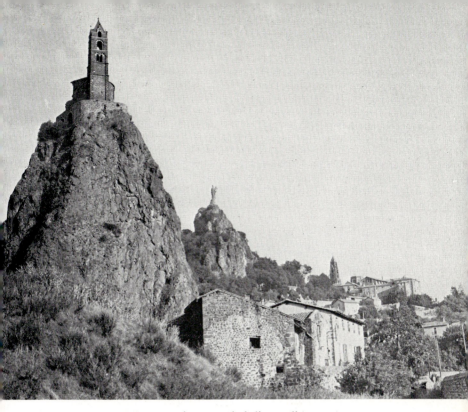

Le Puy; Pic de St Michel d'Aiguilhe

Polignac, the château and the village

Lavoûte Polignac; castle on the Loire

warm-pink tiled roofs give it a certain meridional air: a trait far less marked at Le Puy, further south, where the people, though equally courteous, are less open. Originally a Roman city of some renown, Brioude's position on the plain near the Allier and on the *Voie Rigordane*, the principal trading-route from the Midi to the North, always made it an important *entrepôt* for merchandise from less accessible towns like St Flour and La Chaise-Dieu.

Perhaps this is what brought to Brioude the most celebrated tobacco smuggler of the eighteenth century, one Mandrin, a well-known figure in the folk-lore of this part of the Auvergne. No furtive fly-by-night, Mandrin was accustomed to travelling around with some fifty henchmen, which no doubt ensured his being able to trade in broad daylight. About 1755, he arrived in Brioude after some profitable dealing at Ambert and exacted 15,000 *livres* from the local customs and excise official whom he 'persuaded' to take in a large quantity of tobacco which he could sell privately at contraband prices in order to raise the sum, payable on the smuggler's return! Sadly — for he seems to have been an engaging character who treated with scrupulous honesty, the small traders and inn-keepers with whom he dealt — Mandrin came to a hideous end: the authorities eventually took umbrage at such open tax-evasion, pursued him across the mountains with a small army of enforcement-officers, cornered him in Savoy and brought him back to Valence where he was convicted and broken on the wheel. An unnecessarily harsh punishment, it naturally made of him the folk-hero he has remained ever since.

The high plateau contained by the triangle of *grandes routes* west of Brioude is rich farming land but the villages have little of interest except the huge château of Paulhac, immaculately restored in the sixteenth-century style, and massively dominant on its rock-shelf above the village, behind a crenellated outer wall. It has belonged for generations to the de Miramon family whose children — the locals informed me — "go to England in summer". When I informed them that I was English their polite incredulity might have been taken to indicate — 'Ah! see what such unnecessary expenditure on education brings in its train'. The next village, Beaumont, has a less formidable but still charming essay in restoration, a feudal castle with cropped towers, prettily patched and mended, and a most English-looking garden complete with lawn and terrace stretching down to the road.

The main reason for crossing this plateau, however, is to visit Léotoing and Blesle, the former undoubtedly rivalling the ancient stronghold of the Polignacs for the title of the most photogenic ruin outside the Cantal. I am evidently not alone in thinking so; a bearded, rather professional Frenchman was busily engaged in 'directing' his languid but handsome family into suitable poses when I visited the castle one August afternoon. When they had gone, Léotoing reassumed the sundrowsed silence it has crumbled through these past few hundred years. History is reticent upon the place but it must have been a key-point in the fourteenth century, when it was built, for it commands the road down the Alagnon valley at a strategic bend in the river, as well as the plateau behind. Merle could probably have taken it without too much expenditure of energy (men's lives he did not hold too dearly) since the approaches to the east are flat enough for him to have deployed his artillery. But even he could not have attempted the north-west side for the drop is sheer. The best view of the castle is from just past the bridge on the road to Ardes, on the west side of the river. Léotoing village has the same crumbling yet time-resistant quality. An old lady to whom I gave the time of day nodded with the air of faint alarm one might award a revenant from the past. Perhaps she thought I might be a late arrival from among those other 'English' who marauded these parts when Léotoing's huge *donjon* was still whole (they were usually Gascons, in fact, but one did not stop to ask such things if one's throat were liable to be cut). I had intended to ask for the key to the church, which looks interesting.

Torsiac, the blue-roofed château upon which Léotoing looks arrogantly down, is extremely private. A narrow road climbs sharply through its woods in the direction of Ardes, a thriving holiday-town with a fine church down by the river and what seems, at first sight, an amazingly well-preserved Gothic manor on the main street. It is, in fact, good pastiche. Beyond Ardes lies the Vallée des Rentières, above whose richly wooded slopes hangs like a carious, unpulled tooth, the tower of a medieval stronghold of the Mercoeur brood. Richelieu wisely had it destroyed. Right at the top of this valley, in the fields some little distance from the village, St Alyre-ès-Montagne has a distinctly interesting primitive Romanesque church built of the impermeable and very hard to carve grainy granite the country builders often had to use. Above St Alyre begins that very high plateau I have already described, whose chief market-town is Besse-en-Chandesse.

We can return by the valley of the other Couze, named after Ardes, to take in St Gervazy, quite the sleepiest hamlet one can imagine, like an indistinct murmur from the past barely heard through a half-open door; a shored-up rustic castle in whose courtyard chickens briskly rummage the hard earth while a family of cats sleeps away the daylight hours; a tiny hump-backed bridge much too narrow even for a farm-cart — which the road now ignores — and several tumble-down houses that invite restoration by anyone with a taste for long bucolic summers. The place should be visited, however, for the exquisite twelfth-century statue of the Virgin and Child quite unlike any other in the Auvergne; an elegant upright figure in dark wood which has nothing of the idol about it, but an aristocratic simplicity perfectly created by the rippling stylisation of the gown, finely pleated and with full sleeves hanging to the knees. The face, with its strong faintly aquiline nose, dimpled chin and thin lips curving mournfully at the corners, is neatly framed by a wimple whose wavy edge serves to emphasise the straight, imperious brows. The child, too, has nothing of sweetness or complacence but a prematurely aged awareness; the eyes staring blankly into the future are wide-open — unlike the Mother's which are half-closed against that painful time. The only jarring detail is the fingers, grotesquely long like skeletal claws, surely a concession to the religious tradition which demanded this trait. All in all, a remarkable piece of carving that stays in the mind long after more celebrated portrayals have gone. The only one comparable for intensity of expression is 'Notre Dame de Ronzières', 'discovered' by a draft-ox that obstinately refused to budge until the statue was dug out from between its planted hooves. But she is a true cult-figure with an enormous, skull-capped head, powerful and matronal in her blue country-robe; and her Child a plump, apple cheeked infant whose expression has no mystic foreknowing in it at all.

Blesle is *mignonne*, as befits a place once entirely ruled by women. In the middle of the ninth century the wife of Bernard Plantevelue, Comte d'Auvergne, founded a nunnery here and ordained that the abbesses should — if one may so put it — overlord the town. The best approach is along the D.8 from Anzat-le-Luguet for it enables one to appreciate the cloistered, comfortable situation, enfolded by a bluff which shelters without dominating the houses below. Only two lopped towers at the foot of the hill recall a later, more warlike time when the barons of Mercoeur occupied Blesle and gradually deprived the Mother Superior of her feudal rights. Beyond these towers an unusually wide main street curves gently to the fast-running Voirèze; opening off this street, the Place du Vallat interlocks as it were, into the Place de l'Eglise St Pierre. This church is worth at least an hour for it contains a wealth of interesting things. But do not neglect the lower town; the stream bordering it creates a delightful arrangement of tiny bridges and dark-brown houses, the water dancing in and out of the sun-dappled shadow of its overhanging trees. There are few places in the Auvergne so mellow and coyly domestic as this one: one can almost forget both mountains and marauders for once, only to be recalled to the military past by a street named the rue des Anglais. Mistakenly so as it happens, for the street is called after a convent of English nuns who settled here. The bell-tower of St Martin, nearby, had a church attached until 1793, and just for good measure the Revolutionaries who destroyed it also pulled down the bell tower of the abbey-church of St Pierre.

Returning to it, one notices at once the fine portal with animals and birds climbing around the arch; there is a similar one at Mauriac in the Cantal. The body of the church is very wide and paved with large blocks of stone; below it is a catacomb in which all the Mother Superiors and priests were buried. For the art-historically minded the capital decoration in the *chevet* (or apsidal end) of this church is seen as the beginning of the decadence of Romanesque carving though Focillon, one great authority, prefers to call it "the Baroque phase". He believes these capitals were carved by pupils of the sculptors at Lavaudieu, who were also responsible for the decoration of the southern chapels here. Luxuriant and entertaining as it is, this later work does tend towards decoration for decoration's sake: indeed, if one looks closely, one can see that most of it serves no functional purpose in supporting the arches, being there merely to please the eye. However, the stalls of the *Choeur des Dames* have some fine miséricord seats while the treasury (one has to find the curator) should on no account be missed. Quite often such places contain one or two good things but the riches here no doubt reflect the wealth of this 'priory-town' as a whole: a good twelfth-Century Virgin, an even finer fifteenth-century Virgin and Child in box-wood, a Christ who — though minus his arms — at least echoes in the treatment of the face and hair the exquisite one of Auzon, and a really excellent collection of seventeenth- and eighteenth-century vestments, very well preserved, are only the best items. There are, also, several portraits of former abbesses whose comfortable, unascetic faces illustrate better than anything the easy-going nature of the life of these 'ladies in retirement'. Good works they may have practised, but a little social gossip would not have come amiss. And if Ninon de Lenclos — perhaps the most celebrated and charming of the professional ladies about the court of Louis XIII — really came here to test the attractions of the religious life, they will have had plenty to gossip about.

If I have not sung the praises of gorge-roads it is because I prefer upland ones for their views. Let no-one despise the main road to Massiac, down the *gorges d'Alagnon*, especially in autumn when beech, oak and chestnut trees are in full blaze. Massiac itself is a commercial sort of place now, with a rather too obvious ambition to become a holiday-centre. Yet it was once the seat of a remarkable character who epitomises the unruly yet oddly endearing qualities of the lesser nobility in decline.

Gaspard d'Espinchal was one of those handsome, charismatic people feared by their social equals and admired by women: "tall of stature, of ruddy complexion, his hair falling in curls about his face" (writes his biographer) he was undoubtedly the toast of Clermont in 1652, at the age of 34, when he returned from the civil broils in Gascony that troubled the early years of Louis XIV. He already had a wife tucked away in Massiac but took little care of his lands there except, since court pleasures were expensive, to extort the utmost from them in rents. Moreover, always an aggressive young man of whom his mother had soon despaired, he already had a murder to account for. Rightly wary of Cardinal Richelieu's active disapproval of the unemployed nobility, he decided in 1639 to take service with a sea-going uncle then with the French fleet at Naples. On his way across the Vivarais, however, he chanced to meet, in a forest clearing, a party of young men one of whom had insulted him on a previous occasion; so Gaspard rode straight up to him, shot him dead and galloped away for dear life in the direction of the Rhone valley.

Little came of his naval career for the fighting was over when he arrived in Naples. By the time he returned, however, court-life had sobered, while a rumour reached him that during his absence his wife, of the distinguished and locally powerful family of Châteaumorand, had been unfaithful to him with his bailiff. Riding furiously back to Massiac, he kicked open the door of his sick wife's room and found — no-one but her; the bailiff, guilty or not, had wisely fled to the mountains.

To narrate the life-story of this violent but able man would take too long, yet his career is so vividly evocative of the life of his time in the Auvergne that the reader will pardon a brief résumé. The 'fifties were unfortunate for Gaspard: his father-in-law sued him over his treatment of his daughter and abuse of her dowry while the tenantry on his estates, becoming less and less inclined — at the instigation of the King's *Intendant* — to put up with illegal exactions and petty injustices, stoutly resisted his violent behaviour. In 1662 (by which time his wife, Hélène, had long since retired to the peace of a convent) the Paris *Parlement* decided Gaspard should return her dowry; and at Riom the courts condemned him on various counts, ordering his castles to be rased and imposing heavy fines and restitution of damages to the church the bourgeois of Massiac. Also that "his woods should be cut down to waist-height" — a peculiarly stupid penalty, on the face of it. However, Gaspard was so greatly feared that no-one made any move to carry out these sentences! The following year he elected to appeal to the King in person. But scarcely had he arrived in Paris than, all too typically, he fell foul of the King's chief minister, Colbert, a man who intensely disliked turbulent country nobles. Worse, *Les Grands Jours d'Auvergne* were always in preparation. Our hero, getting wind of this, decided Massiac might be safer, only to discover that the relatives of a girl he had — quite literally — picked from the brambles one day while out riding, were after his blood. In the ensuing brawls an old enemy was shot by one of Gaspard's servants and the Indendant seized the opportunity to declare the Baron d'Espinchal an outlaw. He fled but found a protector in the royal governor of the Forez and so survived once more.

Nemesis finally struck when the 'Grands Jours' came to Clermont. Gaspard's biographer paints a rather pathetic pre-Napoleonic picture of him huddled in his cloak, "crossing, from farm to farm, the snows of the Cantal, followed by a few faithful men . . ." He was making for the fastnesses of the upper Dordogne, a savage country indeed at that time. At any rate, he got away into exile abroad.

An eminently moral tale, the reader might observe, with a sad but most appropriate ending. Not so. Gaspard took service with the Elector of Bavaria, fought successfully against French armies, regained favour with King Louis XIV by helping to arrange a royal marraige and eventually returned to Paris to receive the royal pardon. Richly rewarded, he returned to Massiac once more to rebuild his castle in late seventeenth-century style. In 1686 he made his will, leaving money to the Church at Massiac and Brioude and died in 1690. His wife survived him by ten years, reflecting no doubt upon the ironies of this world.

Massiac, always a fertile place and a market-centre, kept a certain reputation for convivial violence until well into the nineteenth century. *"En ce pays plantureux"*, noted Pourrat, *"on avait trop de sang sous les ongles"*. There was a celebrated fair in June which reached its climax, as so often in the Auvergne, on the eve of St Jean, Midsummer-night. Quite early in the proceedings an elected 'jester', who paid dearly for the privilege in money and in kind, selected a cow for the ultimate feasting and tied it to a stake in someone's field; and this sacrifice was duly 'bled' as a preliminary to the feasting. The following day, a "grand and magnificent procession" made its way noisily to the little 'Chapelle de la Madeleine' which still stands on the western spur of the hill overlooking the town. Here Mass was heard (or rather not heard because the crowd made such a racket) after which the people fell to and ate the celebrated *boeuf aux herbes*. Sadly, the church authorities finally so disapproved of this pagan revel as to forbid it. "They reformed, they suppressed", Pourrat succintly notes; but concludes, if I may freely translate him, with a lament for the passing of the kind of broth of a boy who made himself the life and soul of such parties.

One has a grand view from the chapel, but the road up to it is abominable. From Massiac there is a fine upland road via La-Chapelle-Laurent and Ally to Lavoûte-Chilhac, situated on a narrow plain where the gorge of the Allier opens out briefly before closing again after Langeac. Lavoûte, until it became depopulated in the nineteenth century, had a reputation as a cultured place; St Odilon de Mercoeur, eleventh-century Abbot of Cluny — one of the few admirable men of that rowdy line — was born here, but the abbey buildings are now secular and the great church beside the tower had a somewhat forlorn air. The capitals are interesting. The bridge, very old and restored in the fifteenth century, is extremely handsome. Down river perches St Ilpize, quite a discovery so far as I am concerned since the guides make little of it. Surprisingly so, for the village is spectacularly set on a steep hillside directly above the right bank of the Allier and well repays the walk up to the church and to the ruined castle still higher, in forlorn isolation on a circular mound. From the walls this would appear to have been a Carolingian *château-fort*. The view is magnificent. The village itself evidently fell into serious dilapidation over the years but people are beginning to restore the houses and one can only hope that this fascinating site will be completely reclaimed; it would make a wonderful holiday centre for children. When I inquired why the place was so little known, one local man told me the tourist authorities at Brioude only directed visitors along the main road to Le Puy! Villeneuve, across the dainty little suspension bridge, has several hotels and I noticed people bathing in the Allier, down river.

These gorges are, in fact, relatively little known and we shall explore them in the next chapter on the Velay and on the plateau country to the west of the Allier, called La Margeride.

VII

THE VELAY AND THE MARGERIDE.

The Department of the Haute-Loire is cut — as if with the jagged slash of a giant butcher's knife — by the upper gorges of the Loire: these begin above Retournac, where the river swings sharply west only to turn south again near Vorey and pursue an erratic, winding course towards Le Puy; but it just misses that city, presumably because Le Puy is built upon strata firm enough to resist the folding pressures which created the rift valley the Loire now follows. Below Le Puy the gorges are difficult of access until the river narrows abruptly beyond Solignac and is joined by its main tributary, the Gazelle, on which the former abbey-settlement of Monastier stands. The country east of the Loire we shall ignore since it is not, historically, part of our region.

The central area of rolling hills between the Loire and the Allier, known as the Velay, was the 'kingdom' of the Polignacs until that tempestuous family, recognising forces of social and political change even stronger than themselves, became resigned to a more than nominal allegiance to the Bourbon court. The hills of the Velay merge almost imperceptibly into the Monts du Deves, yet another geological thrust which falls steeply to the upper gorges of the Allier; these are very beautiful and, as yet, singularly wild and unspoiled. West of the Allier rises the broad plateau of the Margeride, a gaunt, boulder-strewn and sparsely populated land from whose northern marches — now thickly forested with pines and firs — the Resistance groups of the Massif Central harried the Nazi Occupation armies.

This whole region, with the exception of Le Puy whose spiky pinnacles crowned by statue or chapel so amaze north European holiday-makers speeding south to the Mediterranean, is little known except to French people of the middle-bourgeois kind, who find the hotels cheap and hospitable to young families, and the countryside both scenically attractive and easily accessible. It is, if anything, more secretive and bland towards the casual visitor than the Basse-Auvergne; certainly, the people are less extrovert and business-like than the *Cantaliens* to the west. There is a heritage of poverty, for the land is not easily worked and Vellave families (they are highly Catholic) were large. In the nineteenth and early twentieth centuries, as the lace-making industry of Le Puy declined, emigration — mostly to St Etienne and Lyon rather than to Clermont — constantly drained the villages of young people eager for a less restricted life. Brioude, essentially commercial and outward-looking, is not typical of the Haute-Loire at all; which is why I included it in the previous chapter.

Apart from Le Puy, famous as a centre of the Marian cult long before St Louis brought to its cathedral the 'Black Virgin' from the Holy Land, the region's history is not well documented; only St Paulien, the first seat of the bishopric of Velay and before that a Gallo-Roman settlement of some note, rates more than a few lines in a factual guide like Kléber-Colombes. This chapter will therefore be relatively short. Yet if peace and scenic beauty and, at the end of the day, a competent and unofficious hospitality are what the traveller requires, both the Velay and the gorge-country of the big rivers are deeply rewarding.

From Brioude, along one of the few straight, fast roads in the Auvergne, do not go so fast that you miss the turn for the château of Chavaniac-Lafayette in the village of St Georges d'Aurac, whose huge parish-church flanks a handy car-park. Basically fourteenth century, this church contains a good statue of St Anne and a delightfully nonchalant one of St George, scarcely deigning to glance at the curly dragon his lance menaces, while his horse, ears most realistically laid back, seems to take a poor view of the whole business. There are, too, a pair of beautifully carved wooden candelabra whose rims carry symbols of the four evangelists and a carved *bénitier* supported by a distinctly odd quartet of angels, their heads far too big for their bodies. Wood carving in this area (as well as in the Cantal) is always worth examining.

Chavaniac, birthplace of the famous marquis who fought in the American War of Independence and supported his own native revolution in its early period, is now an American charitable foundation. Of the original fourteenth-century castle virtually nothing remains: the building was reconstructed twice in the eighteenth century and again in the twentieth. What we see is a long low building with portly towers at either end, and its rather studious, collegiate air is heightened by neat lawns and precisely trimmed evergreens. The interior, quietly elegant but a trifle anonymous, contains some handsome furniture, the bed in which the general was born, and a room full of 1914-1918 war souvenirs and documents. Frankly, the gardens are more interesting — a sophisticated but not too formal translation of the surrounding countryside, which is thickly-wooded and fertile, lyrical rather than grand. The place can only be visited on certain days so it is better to inquire beforehand. The lady who shows one round the house has a severe, matronly air but is extremely informative. The adjoining buildings, off the courtyard, are the dormitories for a colony of deprived children. I asked whether they were free to roam these delightful grounds. "Ah, no!" she replied, "that would scarcely be practical . . ." No doubt she is right, but it seemed a pity. I could not help wondering whether the Comtesse de la Vergne, born Marie-Madeleine de La Fayette, author of that most austerely moral yet humanly intriguing of early French novels, *La Princess de Clèves*, might not have shown herself more liberal in this respect.

Whatever one may think of the somewhat equivocal Marie-Jean-Paul who abandoned the Revolutionary cause, the La Fayette, a distinguished family, served the Auvergne well: the most notable was Gilbert, a *maréchal de France* who served throughout the latter part of the Hundred Years' War, was captured by the English at Verneuil in 1424, ransomed and promised part of the lands of his uncle, the duc de Berry. When hostilities ceased Gilbert helped to put down brigandage and was given the wardship of the young Dauphin, Prince Charles. He eventually went into pious retirement, to be entombed in a chapel at La Chaise-Dieu which he himself had founded. It is pleasant to remember an able and humanly attractive man among the rowdy, ambitiously assertive Auvergnat nobility.

Just below Chavaniac, towards Paulhaguet, is the five-towered, machicholated château of Flaghac, birthplace of Louise, who tamed the unruly Christophe d'Allègre we encounted at Cordes. Quite the prettiest and, architecturally, the most original of the castles round here, it cannot unfortunately be visited.

Rochelambert can, and is well worth the trouble. A few kilometres from St Paulien, off the D.13, it is delightfully situated above a narrow and sinuous valley through which a stream, shadowed by willows and walnut-trees, chuckles over a series of miniature waterfalls. Beside this stream are traces of the Roman road — still crossed by a medieval bridge — built by Agrippa and later followed by pilgrims on their way to Le Puy and Santiago da Compostella. The castle itself, rebuilt after being sacked by soldiers of des Adrets, the villain of La Chaise-Dieu, is so tightly clasped into the shoulder of a wooded basalt cliff as scarcely to be visible on an overcast day; it is, in fact, built of the same ruddy-brown lava, the shade of burnt brick. The approach, down a narrow lane quite overshadowed by trees, adds to the little castle's air of fugitive rusticity so that one is not surprised to learn that it provided the setting for Georges Sand's romantic historical novel, *Jean de la Roche*. The novelist was at school in Paris "*à un couvent des dames anglaises*", with Apollonie de Bruges, the future Marquise de la Rochelambert; the ties then formed were never quite broken and one of Apollonie's daughters was the model for the heroine of another romance, *Valentine*. George Sand visited the castle in 1859, when the Marquise was away, accompanied by a young actress friend and a Monsieur de Manceau — '*l'ami de la fin*', as the French discreetly put it. Their signatures can be seen in the distinguished-visitors book of the château.

Apart from the brutal assault by des Adrets, the castle appears to have enjoyed an untroubled history although an early Seigneur, Roger, was forced to entail it in order to go on St Louis's crusade to the Holy Land. More typical of the place is the tale of the talkative Mme de la Bedoyère, one of the six daughters of Georges Sand's friend. At a royal reception, Madame de la Bedoyère — as famous for her beauty as for her gaffes — turned to her neighbour, a recently appointed Minister, and asked: "Who is that plump little thing over there?" To which the Minister, smiling, replied — "That is my wife, Madame". Moving away, Madame then twittered out this story to a group of amused friends, only to hear the same bland voice at her elbow: "And I, Madame, had the honour to reply . . ."

Rochelambert remained in the family until 1905. The present owner has restored it in excellent taste and the interior is unusually rich in *objets d'art* and period furniture. There is a room full of excellent religious sculpture including two fine Romanesque Madonnas, another in the fourteenth-century style of 'Notre Dame de Marthuret' at Riom, and a curious version — said to be German but modelled on an Italian original — of Christ seated on an ass. Most interesting of all, perhaps, in view of the castle's strategic position overlooking a pilgrim's way, is the leather-belt of the kind traditionally worn by travellers to St James of Compostella; it is hung with cockle-shells, emblem of St James, each one representing in miniature an important stage on the journey. On the way out notice — if you have not already done so — the handsome portal emblazoned with the arms of François de la Rochelambert and his wife, Hélène de l'Estrange, who rebuilt the place in the late sixteenth century: his motto says — "Love or War — Make me worthy, God": and hers — "Neither fear nor envy". The little terrace-garden, whose embrasured wall looks over water-meadows to the gaily hastening stream, adds a final touch of charm. *Un bijou à l'air bien Sandesque*, to coin a phrase.

St Paulien still has the look of the regional capital it once was: the houses are solidly built and the whole place has a square-set, no-nonsense atmosphere about it. Known in Roman times as *Ruessium* it was situated on Agrippa's *Via Bolena*, which follows the river Borne across to Rochelambert. The vast church in the market square looks Romanesque, and was, in fact, built in the twelfth century; but one immediately notices that the apse has been tampered with while the addition of buttresses does not add to the overall effect. Apparently the church was fortified at the time of the Religious Wars, which accounts for the big arcade built out from the west end; and because of the massive buttresses on each flank it still wears an embattled look. However, the austerity of its exterior is lightened by the mosaic effect of the many different shades of stone employed, ranging from light fawn to near black — a quality shared by most churches of the Velay and Loire gorges. On the north side is a grave stele taken from a monument erected by "Rufinus Marius" to his wife. The interior is striking for its width: the original three naves typical

of Auvergnat Romanesque have disappeared as the result of a
seventeenth-century reconstruction after the central vault fell in,
so that the body of the church now resembles one of those hall-
like basilicas found in Sicily and Ravenna. Not all the chapels are
Romanesque (the northernmost is fifteenth-century and that of
the Polignacs on the south side seventeenth) but the second one
to the south has two fascinating capitals that at once recall the
Auvergne; three long-necked heads poking out of foliage on one
and the usurer, totting up his accounts in a book, while demons
hover about him, expectant of the wrath to come, on the other.

Up the road to Chaise-Dieu, on the right, is another reminder
of the village's important past — the delicately sculptured
Romanesque portal of the 'Chapelle des Soeurs-Joseph'. The
fertile country on either side of this road offers several interesting
villages, notably St Geneys, once a fortified *enceinte*, which has a
tall, sober *manoir* with brown-stone crenellation, and
encorbelment at each corner. When I was there a bulldozer was
rattling about the garden and the house, whose western balconies
command a delightful outlook, had a deserted air. Between here
and Bellevue the road climbs steadily to afford some fabulous
glimpses of the craggy hills above the Loire. Bellevue is pretty,
especially along the lanes leading off behind the church, but
Chomelix is more interesting; on the buttresses at the apsidal end
of its thirteenth-century church crouch gargoyle figures with
huge cannon-balls in their mouths, as if ready to drop them on
any marauder from the east, while the interior contains an
attractively painted font with fine ram's head decoration and a
proud collection of heraldic roof-bosses in the south chapels.
Both Chomelix and Sanssac, nearby, are of Gallo-Roman origin.
The upland road from Chomelix to Chamalières, in the Loire
valley, offers more excellent views and a glimpse of the ruined
castle of Chalençon off to the left. But let us leave Chamalières
and its abbey-church for the moment and return to Polignac, just
off the D.13 from St Paulien to Le Puy; for this is the most
startling and evocative ruin in the Velay and one that offers a
most interesting insight into the history of the region.

If ever a ruined site echoed hollowly to the sound of trumpets
long ago it is the abandoned Château de Polignac: I first saw it
on a rather stormy October day when the enormous *butte,*
weathered a tawny, leonine colour by sun and wind, so blended

into the autumnal russets of the hill behind as to seem deliberately camouflaged; the curious formation of the rocks on its western face lent the impression that the houses below continue up its sheer slope to form a complete medieval village (the *butte* is crowned by a single square *donjon*-tower often glimpsed, tantalisingly, through gaps in the hills to the east). In spring or early summer, when the countryside is green, one perceives more clearly the splendidly arrogant isolation of the site; a natural fortress that no medieval baron, let alone a Polignac, could have afforded to neglect. Possessing it, kings they were in fact if not in name. No-one ever took the place.

The Emperor Claudius, lame, wife-ridden, erudite, came here, perhaps to consult the oracle of Apollo for insight into his troubles. He will scarcely have been deceived by the crooked priests who listened through an echo-chamber to the muttered prayers of pilgrims below; and then, while the suppliant sweated up the rock-strewn scarp, prepared their answer in the temple above and spoke it through the mouth of the god as he knelt at its feet. The modern traveller will not come this way without climbing-boots. The conventional approach leads up from the little square above the hotels (most of the village lies behind the *butte*) on the eastern slope. Immediately, the extent of the place is apparent although practically all the buildings have disappeared leaving only the great tower, built between 1385 and 1421, and some fifteenth- and seventeenth-century remains to the south. The tower is worth climbing for the view, with the Pic de Lizieux and Mont Meygal, both well over 4,000 feet, clearly visible beyond the Loire; to the south-west Le Puy is hidden by the hill on which captured English soldiers were hung by a fourteenth-century vicomte. On the first floor lies the huge masque of Apollo, so called; it looks more like a head of Jupiter or Neptune to me as I never saw a bearded Apollo. The archer-slits on the walls on the north side are of an inverted-key form, very rare if not unique.

The rest has to be peopled by the imagination. The Polignacs, having opted for respectability, abandoned this castle in the seventeenth century and retired to their other seat at Lavoûte-Polignac on the Loire, a *plaisance* rather than a fortress. This in itself makes a valuable point: the history of the family becomes political and social, not military. The soldiers, as I have suggested, were a very mixed bunch: one of the most infamous, Héracles — classical first names no doubt invoked the family's claim to descent from high priets of Apollo — so overstepped the flexible morality of his time that he was condemned by a council of bishops at Le Puy to go barefoot to Brioude. Here he was soundly whipped for his pains by a soldier-monk. Another late fourteenth-century vicomte brutally put down the *Tuchins*, a movement of peasant revolt whose origins lay in the people's resentment at the royal government's inability to get rid of unemployed soldiers who had lapsed into brigandage. Eventually, it was Bertrand du Guesclin, the only general of true genius the French produced during the Hundred Years' War, who swept this country clear of looters, only to be fatally wounded besieging Randan at the foot of the Margeride. Du Guesclin's embalmed remains were brought back to Le Puy and buried there.

Polignac, then, represents the naughty history of the Velay. That this part of France remained so long a remote, misgoverned province is largely due to its unprincipled adventurers, yet the city itself retains to this day a certain air of withdrawn piety. The main shopping streets are ugly and architecturally rather dull, while the *grande place* has suffered the fate of many squares and become a huge car-park. Penetrate the streets above it, and to the south towards the river, and the city's true character is revealed: sober, pious, typically secretive, quite in contrast to bustling Brioude and busy Issoire. Characteristically, the great cathedral does not show itself until one climbs the hill, as if it, too were determined not to obtrude upon the visitor.

Pierre d'Estienne in his excellent book upon the development of the cities of the Massif Central makes the point that Le Puy still suffers from remoteness from Paris and a lack of local markets for its products. Furthermore, he remarks — "The story of Le Puy is that it has often directed its efforts towards the manufacture of cheap products whose marketing suffers greatly from the town's isolation and difficulty of access in the heart of the Massif Central"; and he cites the lace-industry, highly prosperous in the fifteenth and sixteenth centuries, which failed to move with the times, paid low wages and so could attract neither capital nor skilled labour with which to start new factories once the 'cottage industry' network declined. Even in the eighteenth century most of the lace was exported not to Paris or the Midi but to Spain. And this market was closed in 1954. The leather industry (the local *vachette du Velay* is well-known for the quality of her hide) has also failed to develop for much the same reason.

Nevertheless, in the little shops of the lanes leading up to the 'HauteVille' the persistent shopper can find some interesting things, mostly in ironwork or leather. The great festival of Notre-Dame du Puy in mid-August still brings thousands of pilgrims to the town and must contribute greatly to its apparent prosperity. The cathedral itself, hemmed in by Bishop's Palace and cloister, is best seen from above, from the Rocher Corneille or from the pinnacle crowned by St Michel d'Aigulhe. The main west door is approached, now, by a grand stairway; for the weary pilgrims of the Middle Ages this final climb, after the long journey across the mountains, must have seemed mighty steep. It still has to be taken slowly!

The interior is rather dark but extremely grand, the nave sweeping down in a series of shallow domes supported by the Byzantinesque *squinches* — niches with semi-domes — which help to give the building its Southern Spanish air. The proportions are good and if the total effect is less than noble this is probably due to the huge organ that blocks the east end, to the dreadful Baroque excrescence on the last double-arch and to the darkness of the transept chapels. Compared with Notre Dame du Port at Clermont, or with Brioude, the interior also lacks harmony and that variety of spatial perspective peculiar to the Romanesque. The Black Virgin is not the one given by St Louis, which was publicly burned during the Revolution. There are some good chasubles and communion-cups in the sacristy, a fine bronze head of Christ and an eighteenth-century Crucifixion less mannered than most of its kind. By far the best part of the cathedral, however, is the cloister and here the Spanish or 'Mozarab' decoration which distinguishes Le Puy is seen to fine effect in the polychrome stonework of the shallow arches, the delicate treatment of the cornices above them and the restful yet elegant styling of the supporting columns, their capitals richly carved in foliate and floral designs. The singularity of this architecture resides in its use of the true compass-drawn half-circle, whose geometrical precision the builder undoubtedly took from Moorish models, whether or not he had visited the Mohammedan parts of Spain. Which is quite possible since merchants and craftsmen from the Massif Central passed constantly across the Pyrenees. Many people emigrated to Spain during the guerrilla-wars of the fourteenth and fifteenth centuries. Yet another 'Mozarab' feature of the Cathedral is the Kufic inscriptions on the portals, so that it may be seen not, indeed, as an imitation of Moorish architecture but of the cultural diffusion of decorative motifs adapted to a fundamentally Romanesque building.

The curious may wish to climb the interior of the fifty-foot high statue called Notre-Dame-de-France, on the Rocher Corneille — more rewarding is the Chapel of St Michel d'Aigulhe on the northern pinnacle. The worship of the Black Virgin and her Christian predecessors probably replaced that of an Earth-Mother cult; and there are traces of a temple to Mercury, the messenger-god of trade — another familiar pagan cult in the Avergne — on this volcanic pinnacle. The chapel, quaintly and ingeniously adapted to the restrictions of the site, was built towards the end of the eleventh century: its arabesque decoration and the trilobate treatment of the portal confirm the southern Spanish influence in the basilica.

A pleasant drive down-river along the steep-sided gorge brings one to Lavoûte-sur-Loire. The Polignac *plaisance* is sweetly perched on a spur of rock right above the river. Monks from Noirmoutier, near the mouth of the Loire, took refuge from the Normans here in the ninth century, bringing with them the relics of St Philibert. Afterwards, a medieval castle was established of which the massive gateway at the garden-entrance is all that remains.

The grandson of its first recorded occupant, a bishop of Le Puy, also took to the religious life as a knight of St Julien de Brioude. His tomb had a curious history. Demolished during the Revolutionary troubles, only the cover and its effigy survived; but this had apparently been subject to superstitious practices on the part of pregnant women who came to ask its help to give them a sage delivery — for which a zealous church-helper destroyed it in 1850. Between the pious and the improper whose remains shall rest in peace? Another intriguing story is told of Claude-Armand, Vicomte de Polignac in the late fifteenth century. He was returning to the castle along a road above Chamalières when a member of his suite begged him to make a detour to the famous abbey there, where he might pray before a nail preserved from the Cross. True to type the noble gentleman exclaimed: "If this relic has so much virtue let it bring back the gift of sight to my mule!" The mule did indeed recover its sight; but the vicomte was equally suddenly struck with blindness. Full of remorse, he prostrated himself before the relic, promising the gift of a precious reliquary if his vision was restored. It was; yet history relates the vicomte afterwards suffered both financial and marital misfortunes. Compelled by Louis XI to marry Jacqueline de Chabannes, he 'took tut' and refused to speak a word to his wife, who lived a life of seclusion in another wing of the castle. The couple only met once a week, at Mass on Sundays, when they nodded to each other briefly before kneeling at prayer.

The guide who shows you round the place has the imposing presence of a major-domo, this native dignity enhanced by a dark uniform whose buttons are emblazoned with the family crest. It is a remarkably interesting castle with thirteenth- and fourteenth-century chimneys, two Chinese clocks and a collection of Polignac portraits of unnusually good quality. One of them, surprisingly in such an ultramontane family (the Duc Jules, whose reactionary edicts provoked the Paris Revolution of 1830, was made 'Prince' by the Pope) is of a Protestant ancestor; bearded and a little grim, he has a worried, inward-looking gaze. In the 'grande salle' Protestants and Catholic Leaguers met in 1592 to try and reach agreement: the ensuing peace brought the whole province over to Henri IV.

At Lavoûte, too, was born Cardinal Melchior de Polignac who negotiated the Peace of Utrecht, to end Marlborough's war in 1713: a very cultured man elected to the Académie Française and sometime Ambassador to Poland, to whom Pope Alexander VII remarked: "I don't know how you do it — you always seem to be of my opinion, yet it is I who end by agreeing with yours". The ladies of this period were less fortunate; one of them had an *amitié folle* for Louis XIV, who neglected her, while another, Yolande — the wife of Prince Jules — is thought to have had a bad influence on Marie-Antoinette, who loaded her with jewels and had her husband made a duke.

The little church in Lavoûte-sur-Loire is worth a glance, as is the one in the village of Polignac itself, which has some good frescoes, modern windows portraying the more saintly family ancestors and some fine polychrome statuary.

Further down-river (although, somehow, one seems to be climbing) is Chamalières, easily the best Romanesque church in the region and delightfully situated above the river, behind a huddle of russet-tiled old houses. One wing of the little cloister, quietly mouldering in a profusion of shrubs, grasses and wild flowers, is the only witness to its abbey, founded in the tenth century by the great benedictine monastery at Monastier, which we shall visit. This church has truly noble proportions and some beautiful 'early Norman' — rather than Auvergnat — decoration both inside and out. But it is the site I remember most: the river, quite deep and placid here, winds grandly in the manner of the Dordogne, with a ruined castle on a summit in the middle distance and a background of rugged hills dotted with scrub-oak and small conifers. This must have been a wild place, indeed, until recent times. Now it has a good simple hotel, several restaurants and, as the excellent *Guide Pratique de la Haute-Loire* tells us, is a *paradis des pêcheurs, des chercheurs de champignons et des fruits sauvages*. One is never far from good eating in France.

The country south of Le Puy is even more rugged, tangled by volcanic upheaval into a chaos of deep rift valleys; the peaks, frequently around 3,000 feet, rounded and balding, are less sharply upstanding than the Monts des Dômes and their lower slopes less richly forested though the meadows in the valleys are fertile and well-farmed. There seem to be fewer cattle here, however, and one misses the music of their bells, which makes drowsy summer afternoons in the Cantal so tunefully pleasing.

The road to Monastier-sur-Gazelle passes round Bozouls, a tiny village of steep, cobbled lanes dominated by an immense castle, magnificently sited to dominate the valley of the Loire, some 2,000 feet below. The square 'donjon', one of the largest I have ever seen, stands out against the later buildings, which have a Scots 'baronial' air thanks to their dainty *tourelles*. The list of past *seigneurs* reads like an honours-roll to departed nobility: Polignac succeeds de Chalençon, followed by Beaufort-Turenne, d'Armagnac, La Tour d'Auvergne, de Montaigut . . . even the deputy mayor of Le Puy, who restored Bozouls in 1808, has a triple Christian name and a *de Brive* to crown it.

Monastier-sur-Gazelle was famous for a 'Tuesday Market' established by letters patent from Charles VIII, no less, in 1495; while the abbey, founded by St Calmin in the late seventh century, is quite the oldest in the Velay. At the height of its prestige from the tenth to the fourteenth centuries its dependencies and possessions stretched from Puy de Dôme into Provence and across the Italian border as far as Turin. The decline began with the appointment of the first lay abbot, François d'Estaing, of the branch which owned land round Murol and St Nectaire in the Auvergne. It was he who built the elegant stairway climbing to the west front.

What remains is a huge church, austerely grand inside, richly polychrome outside: the west façade is especially beautiful, with delicate *chevron* colonnettes supporting a striped multi-arched window. The geometric decoration above this is also remarkable, striking the Mauresque note of Le Puy, while the massive power of the building as a whole is enhanced by the deep browns and purple-reds of the local stone. The interior, equally imposing in its height and nobility of proportion, has five apsidal chapels, the best and last-built being the monument, in ornate Renaissance style, of the de Saint-Nectaire family; its ceiling would grace a château on the lower Loire. The treasury has several fine things, including a fifteenth-century painting of the Descent from the Cross which looks Burgundian or Flemish (the donor on the left is the Abbot, Erailh, who contributed largely to this treasury); and a reliquary bust of St Theofrède, nephew of the founder, which, though cruder in workmanship, strongly resembles the exquisite St Baudime in the church at St Nectaire. I also recall a fine primitive 'Crucifixion' in the body of the church and a worn capital showing two curly-horned cows, wide-eyed as if in wonder at being stuck up there, so high, in this grand place.

A narrow upland road across wide, open country leads to Presailles; a little further south, just off the road on a grassy promontory, is the beautifully restored sixteenth-century Chateau de Vachères, many-towered, crenellated, a place of dignified hauteur, like a grey-haired princess some time from court but retaining all her courtly presence. The little guide to the castles of the Haute-Loire remarks that whereas the nobility of the Ile de France tended to pull down their feudal châteaux and build anew in the eighteenth-century style, those of the

Velay preferred to rebuild from the inside, so preserving the feudal exterior but civilising within. Vachères is a fine example of this. Unusually, it is roofed with the grey-green lauze tiles typical of the Auvergne.

Alternatively, from Monastier, there is a main road — very pretty in its later stages — leading south to Pradelles at the extreme edge of the Velay: this by-passes Arlempdes, a weird and haunted medieval village with an eleventh-century gateway and the ruins of a fortress littered about a basalt ledge. Weathering has created skeletal pinnacles and rounded 'pillars' so that, from a certain distance, one cannot be sure which is rock and which is castle. Highly picturesque. But I should prefer not to spend the winter here!

Pradelles, a market town of some size, is both melancholy and charming: melancholy because so many of the old houses in the lower quarter are falling — or have fallen — into ruin, charming because it is all of a piece, dignified even in decay. The extent of its main square would seem to indicate a wealthy past; many of the houses have kept their finely moulded windows and doorways while the Place des Halles keeps one cross-vaulted arcade over the pavement. A place to walk around. I found the little *Oustalou* folk-museum extremely interesting. It contains one of those canopied short beds in which people slept upright, a custom also found in the Basse-Auvergne (there is another example in the museum of Richard-le-Bas, above Ambert).

A few miles north-west of Pradelles the Allier becomes a river rather than a stream, although almost everywhere one has to walk in order to reach it. This is very wild country indeed. The villages do not offer much until one has crossed the Allier, at Pont de Vabres, a point where it is narrow, fast and savagely picturesque. The road turns east after climbing out of the gorge and crosses a ridge before dropping sharply and beautifully to Monistrol d'Allier. I found Monistrol a lovely village, spread about a height dropping sheer to the forested gorge. The belvedere opposite the church, in the upper quarter, provides a magnificent and shady view over the roof-tops and there is one excellent hotel.

The country both north and south of the N.589, crossing the Monts du Devès from Monistrol to Le Puy, is perhaps the least known of all. There are few large villages (the country is sparsely inhabited) so hotel-accommodation is limited to established holiday-centres like Monistrol or the cluster of small places around Chapeauroux in the extreme south, where the Velay borders the Lozère; or at Cayres, just off the 'route nationale' 88 and conveniently close to the tranquil, pine-wooded but rather haunted Lac du Bouchet — the Vellave equivalent of Lac Pavin. The traveller should not be put off, for the landscape is of surpassing beauty and if the hotels are full there is often private accommodation suitable for a short stay. There are fine churches at Sanssac, St Jean Lachalm (very pure Romanesque) and Loudes, while the castles, though I found none that could be visited, are always worth seeking out for their picturesque situation and architectural interest. St Vidal, quite close to Le Puy, off the N.590, and the crag-top ruin of La Rochegude are the outstanding examples.

My own favourite village would be Prades, about half-way between Monistrol and Langeac; here, a tributary stream rushes down to the Allier from the hills to the west and joins it just below a bridge where a small *plage* has been made accessible to bathers. Foreign visitors have discovered this village but it could hardly become spoilt since the site is quite hemmed in by the surrounding hills. Whether walking or driving this is a superb piece of country to explore. Along the gorge-road towards Chanteuges is the tiny village of St Julien-des-Chazes and quite near (on the far bank of the Allier) is a little chapel, St Marie-des-Chazes, which contains a fine Virgin and Child — simple but remarkably handsome for all that. One has to obtain the key to this chapel from the curé at St Julien.

Finally, before we strike west across the high plateau of the Margeride, the great church at Chanteuges should not be missed. Standing on a spur of rock just above the confluence of the Desges and the Allier, it is best approached by car, up the little lane that loops off behind the village; or one may cross the bridge by the main road and make the stiff climb on foot. As might be expected from the size of the church, this was an abbey-foundation dating back to the early tenth century. It flourished for 200 years and then, about 1130, occurred a change of fortune. We are told that a certain Baron Itier, lord of Digons, was in the habit of robbing travellers along the Voie Rigordane, the main road to the south. One day a monk from the abbey went up to the baron's castle to try and persuade him to mend his ways, and was promptly hanged from a nearby tree. Shortly afterwards the baron's only daughter — whom he loved dearly — died suddenly and inexplicably; which he took to be the vengeance of God. So Baron Itier abandoned robbery and became a monk. For a time all went well but past habits proved too strong: not only did he revert to brigandage but enlisted the monks in his band. Such infamy brought down upon Chanteuges the wrath of Etienne de Mercoeur, Superior of the parent abbey of La Chaise Dieu, who laid siege to it and expelled the evil-doers (Itier, however, escaped). Perhaps because it was so isolated, the status of Chanteuges was reduced; it became a priory and the summer resort of the abbots of La Chaise Dieu.

Doubtless, the church fell into some disrepair during the Hundred Years War; but in 1491 an energetic abbot, Jacques de Sennectaire, took such a liking to the place, so beautifully situated overlooking the river, that he restored and embellished it; the vaulted roof, the choir stalls, and the flamboyant east window are his work, and he also rebuilt the cloister and established the chapel of St Anne on its north side. This was closed for restoration when I visited Chanteuges in 1972 but it is said to contain some very beautiful and unusual sixteenth-century sculpture.

The exterior of the church is rugged rather than beautiful and limitations of space evidently prevented any elaborate treatment of the apse. Inside, the grandeur of proportion is striking — more so than at any other Romanesque church except St Julien de Brioude. The plan is basilical rather than typically Auvergnat and despite the great height of the nave there are only four pillars on either side, which adds to the open, hall-like effect. There are too many good things in this church to enumerate but the stall-backs and misericords are of outstanding interest while the capitals on the south side were apparently carved by that late Romanesque school already encountered at Blesle and Brioude. The sixteenth-century pulpit, finely wrought, is emblazoned with the arms of Sennectaire. Comparable in the beauty of its situation with St Saturnin and St Nectaire, the priory church of St Marcellin de Chanteuges, once a halting-place on the pilgrim road to Compostella, is a place that tempts one to linger; the open courtyard on its west side looks down on the hamlet below and there is — as so often in the Auvergne — the excited conversation of waters rushing to a distant sea. Heracleitus observed that the water in a river perpetually changes although the river remains the same. I would like to believe that the withdrawn beauty of this place will not change either, in any permanent sense.

A few kilometres beyond Chanteuges the main road turns abruptly west and climbs steeply to the Margeride through the forests of Pourcheresse: the Puy de Charraix blocks the view towards the Allier but the country opens out towards the west and the high pine-woods about Mont Mouchet. Some fifteen kilometres on is Saugues, a grey-stone, windswept sort of place and the only town of any size for miles in this rocky country of grazing-land and lonely farms. Through Saugues, in the early spring of 1944, quietly trickled the *cadres* of the Vellave Resistance to confront the Germans, at bay at last and concerned to wipe out any large force that might hamper their communications during the expected Allied invasion. More famous still, however, is the gathering that takes place every year on the eve of Good Friday; for Saugues is the scene of one of the very few Processions of the White Penitents to have been maintained down the years since the late fifteenth century. This particular *confrérie* was founded rather later, in 1652, by the Bishop of Mende, capital of the Lozère, to which this area is geographically linked. And since the Procession was approved by Pope Urban VIII soon afterwards, a Chapel of the Penitents, attached to the church in the main square, was then built.

Such processions were not, it seems, intended to convince those of weak belief, still less to frighten them into a more regular observance, but to confirm in the minds of the faithful the sanctity and continuing significance of Christ's Passion. There is nothing outrageous or deliberately theatrical about this procession; it is an act of pious remembrance concerned — regardless of flashing cameras and television-lights — to embody in action the original progress to Golgotha.

Throughout the proceedings the element of participation is important. The afternoon confession of the *Confrères* is, naturally, private; but at six o'clock marchers, congregation and strangers hear the Pascal Mass together in the church. The former then retire to rest and eat a frugal meal while the people take up position on the route traditionally followed round the little town. About eight o'clock, two blows are struck on the door of the Chapel and the first of the marchers appear — the *Mères Chrétiennes* or, as we should probably call them, the Mothers Union attached to the parish-church; they are followed by choir-boys in white surplices carrying the traditional square or hexagonal lanterns whose white glass is painted with emblems of the Passion. Other children of the community join the procession and, on their heels, the first of the white-gowned hooded brothers (called *cagoules*) appears — the standard-bearer, bare-footed and carrying the *gonfalon*, a processional cross swathed in white cloth. He is accompanied by two other brothers, with hoods raised, and then come the first three 'penitents' proper, heads bowed, faces quite concealed beneath lowered hoods, the middle one bearing the Chalice, symbol of Christ's blood, high above his head.

At the centre of the procession, of course, walks the principal figure, a brother in red carrying the great wooden cross itself, bent almost double beneath its weight, helped by 'Simon of Cyrene' who tries to share his burden. Some members of the Order wear gowns with white cord at the waist while another, in a red hood, bears a heavy eight-sided column representing the Flagellation. So the procession winds slowly through the steep, narrow streets of silent, unlit houses, the cool night wind bringing a touch of colour to the pale cheeks of children whose thin voices — chanting prayers and, at certain intervals, the sad words of the *Miserere* — rise above the harsher incantation of the men and the mellow, tender voices of the women. Three times only the long white coil halts a few moments for the principal bearers to take breath and rest, while the crowd nearby breaks into sharp, excited conversation. Finally the great cross is borne to the steps of the altar in the chapel and laid there for the *Confrères* to kneel beside it while they and the crowd, in a last act of ritual participation, sing prayers and psalms together.

A strange survival, one might think, in this region whose people are as renowned for their taciturnity of expression as for a certain emotional reticence not common in the Gallic race. Yet such a ceremony does not seem out of place in high, bleak Saugues at the turning of the year while the snow lingers in sheltered hollows and lies quite thickly on the peaks, a reminder of the 'dead; season shortly to be dissolved in May sunshine and by the first warm rains. Christian ritual in the Auvergne is so often pagan ritual transformed or reborn in new guise; where the winters are hard and the land the only provider, spring festivals carry deep layers of meaning so that we might interpret this ceremony as one of renewal after the long pain of winter. In Combrailles — the thought occurs — they still celebrate the purification of the mother, after she has born her first child; the young woman enters the church at Sunday service but remains by the door. Then the priest comes forward to bless her with holy water; and so she is readmitted into the body of the congregation.

In the little museum which has replaced the foresters' hut in a clearing on Mont Mouchet is the picture of a boy of fourteen or fifteen who ran messages for the Resistance: he was tortured to death by the Gestapo because he would not reveal information which might have led to the capture, and certain death, of his friends. On a little bridge beyond La Besseyre St Mary, as one climbs up to this place, is a plaque to two women, Mélanie and Marguerite Cubizolles, shot by German troops as they passed through. One would not wish to reopen old wounds and it is not for the stranger to moralise in matters over which the French themselves are apt to shrug and turn the conversation. Nevertheless, the events of June 1944 should not be passed over; they are part of our own contemporary history and the cause for which these people died was also ours.

The battle centred here was no ambuscade like that at St Floret, where a lad fired on a German vehicle and some half-dozen citizens were shot in reprisal. 260 men died in and around Mont Mouchet and 180 were wounded; while about 100 hostages were subsequently shot in Murat, near St Flour, and elsewhere. The background is simple enough: word came from England in the spring that the invasion of France was planned, the date decided. In April, at Montluçon, agents of Special Operations Europe met leaders of the Maquis to organise a solid bastion of resistance in the Massif Central that would seriously delay the reinforcement of the German armies in the west. On 15th May at Paulhaguet, a further meeting of Resistance chiefs confirmed these plans and five days later the order went out to mass all available forces, which would gather at Mont Mouchet, already the secret H.Q. for the Massif Central region.

Before the end of May some 2,700 men had come here, mostly from the Py-de-Dôme — by train or lorry, on foot, on bicycles, however they could; and large contingents were forming at Chandes-Aigues on the Truyère, and at St Genest.

The Germans could hardly fail to notice such large movements and by the 2nd June the battle had been joined. Naturally, in such a wild and broken country unsuitable for the German tanks and armoured vehicles, it was a very fluid affair: groups of *maquisards* broke out from St Jean Lachalm and Chaudes-Aigues to join the centre of resistance on Mont Mouchet and there were pitched battles at Clavières above Chandes-Aigures, at Pinols on the main Langeac-St Flour road, and La Vachellerie, near Sauges. Counter-attack followed counter-attack and both sides lost heavily; but the Germans especially so since the French were more mobile and could regroup the more easily.

However, as the Germans had committed over 8,000 men, including infantry, artillery and armoured vehicles, there could be only one result: on the 11th June they surrounded the forest area in which the *maquisards* had concentrated and tried to wipe them out. They did not succeed. When they reached the clearing where the tall grey monument now stands, they found nothing, neither men nor material; in true guerilla fashion the French had melted away to continue the battle in smaller groups in various parts of their mountain-fastness. On the Truyère the battle went on until the 20th June, when 'Colonel Gaspard' (who figures prominently in the film *Le Chagrin et la Pitié*) gave the order to disengage. Overall, German casualities were heavy: the job had been done.

The museum is a sad place, all too evocative of those savage times: Clavières, Paulhac and Lorcières were burnt and the charming little town of Ruynes-sur-Margeride largely destroyed as were many isolated farms in the battle areas. It was raining hard the day I visited Mont Mouchet and mist lay over the pines, a slowly moving shroud. We should not, perhaps, try too hard to remember details of reprisal, of torture, of men and women deported to concentration camps, stamped on their forearms like cattle. Neither should we forget.

In the end — after the recriminations, the private vengeances, the plotting and manoeuvring that always follows great clashes of arms, tolerance prevailed. Let the last word come from a journalist friend of mine in Clermont who was born in the Haute-Loire. When I asked him why men like a certain aristocrat who fought against his own countrymen as an S.S. officer were not courtmartialled and shot in 1945, he smiled reflectively, a trifle sadly, but without bitterness: "Ah! well, you see," he replied, "they thought they were patriots too . . ."

VIII

CANTAL: ST FLOUR TO THE CHESTNUT COUNTRY

The *campagnard cantalien* is a natural aristocrat; ownership of land
gives pride and the cattle he grazes upon it measure his wealth.
Aurillac is the commercial capital of this region (known
traditionally as the 'Haute-Auvergne'), St Flour its spiritual and
judicial centre. Let us begin with St Flour, itself a proud city of
which the saying goes: "None ever took you by force except the
wind!" And this is true, for no-one ever did; not even Merle
though he almost succeeded one August night in 1578. The
townspeople, with the confidence born of several centuries of
fruitless assault, had gone to bed; but one man, the Consul
Brisson, slept nervously enough to be awakened by the faint
scuffle of feet under the ramparts. Hastening outside he ran to the
walls, peered over and saw several Protestant soldiers climbing
up on ladders. He rang the alarm bell and the guard came running
up in the nick of time.

Oddly enough, one can scarcely appreciate the enormous
strength of this site except from the Massiac road at a certain
point on the hill leading out from the lower town. Then it can be
seen that the town is built like a fortress on its promontory of
basalt rock — the drop is sheer on three sides. Indeed, so
prescribed is St Flour by its natural situation it has only been able
to expand by dividing into two, the lower suburb by the river
being largely nineteenth- or twentieth-century. This, fortunately,
has enabled the *Ville-Haute* to retain its character and atmosphere
almost unspoiled so that there are few towns more characteristic
to walk around. The great open space called Les Promenades,
bordered by trees on three sides, was originally cut in half by the
eastern ramparts: from here one passes into the old town. To
describe St Flour as charming would be mildly inaccurate. What
it does have is dignity and, in a quite unselfconscious way, a

certain *hauteur* — a very bourgeois sense of its own importance perhaps. Until the seventeenth century it was ruled by three elected 'consuls' and was noted for a sharply independent attitude towards such grasping aristocrats as the duc de Berry. Architecturally it is not distinguished except for the Maison Consulaire — the former town-hall — off the Place d'Armes, and some fine fifteenth- and sixteenth-century houses in the rue Marchande and the rue du Thuile; but is all of a piece and one grows to like the place after visiting it several times. The famous walls have practically disappeared but there are fine views from wherever one can penetrate to the perimeter of the upper town, especially on the northern and western sides. The main square, the Place des Armes, which has remained virtually intact, is one of the best in the Auvergne and it is unfortunate the cathedral presents so plain a façade for — from the river or the hill looking back to the city — the twin towers peeping above the houses lead one to expect something grander; while the apsidal arrangement, though imposing, is rather spoilt by the buttresses reaching across it and by the lack of any central 'mass' to build up to.

The beginnings were Romanesque: in the mid eleventh century two repentant barons, Amblard de Nonette (who had killed one of his own family) and Astorg d'Apchon — his crime is not recorded — contributed largely towards a priory-church that would replace the oratory dedicated to St Flour, martyred Bishop of the Lodève. Pope Urban II consecrated it in 1095 on his way to preach the first Crusade at Clermont. But, for once, the builders were incompetent and the nave fell down in 1396. As the marauding 'English' were gradually driven from the plains, the new building began to rise although it was not to be completed until some sixty years later, as an inscription on the façade attests. The interior, however, is what we should call 'Early English' rather than fifteenth century — tall, plain to the point of severity, but well-lit by high lancet windows. There was a further restoration in the mid-nineteenth century and this, one feels, must have been for the better: eighteen lateral chapels were cleared from the side-aisles and a screen from the central nave. The church contains many interesting things. In the entrance-porch, below a little 'coffer' hollowed out of stone, an inscription says — *"L'Arche du Bastiment"*; this was the box for contributions towards the new church, and the time this re-building took can no doubt be attributed to the poverty caused by the Hundred Years' War during which some *Sanflorains* despaired sufficiently to emigrate to Spain. Also in the porch is a rather charming sixteenth-century fresco representing souls in purgatory with two outsize angels, like benevolent teachers, shushing them away from the flames.

The best sculpture is undoubtedly the Christ, known as the '*Le Bon Dieu noir*', in the south-aisle; this, though the treatment of the body is more realistic, bears such a close resemblance, in the stylised treatment of the hair, beard and robe, to the beautiful Christ at Auzon that one can scarcely doubt it must be twelfth century or — as the little guide to the church suggests — a very good fifteenth-century copy. At any rate it is extremely moving, quite the best in the Cantal. Equally famous (but not, to my mind, of equal beauty) is the twelfth-century Virgin and Child known as '*Notre Dame des Pegros*'; this statue has a Roman rather than a Romanesque dignity and repose (the eyes do not compel) while the Child has a handsome but somewhat unspiritual face. The curious name '*Pegros*' is probably *languedoc* for '*pieds gros*'. As we have noticed before, hands and feet on such twelfth-century statues are often disproportionately big, a trait intended to emphasise the superhuman quality of the subject. The curious lid-like patch on the Virgin's hair reminds us, too, that these statues often contained relics (St Baudime at St Nectaire is a reliquary bust). Also worth examining are the Pompignac tomb, whose three tiers of stone figures above the finely carved body of the dead Christ portray the Last Judgment, and the little fifteenth-century Pietà, oddly moving in its folk-art simplicity. The Musée de la Haute-Auvergne in the seventeenth-century Bishop's Palace next to the cathedral also merits a visit for a really excellent eleventh-century 'St Pierre' from Bredons, near Murat, paintings by Edward Onslow of the same family that married into the castle at Aultéribe and some interesting documentation on the local Resistance.

The country immediately to the south-west and north-west of St Flour is known as '*La Planèze*' — *planèze* being the dialect word for upland plain. It is a very different country from that of the western part of the Cantal, being relatively unwooded, though the farms often keep a protective coppice of trees around them;

wisely so, for this high country, well over 3,000 feet for the most part, must be very draughty, and it snows a lot in winter. There are few large villages, the farms being dotted about the countryside rather than grouped together as they are in the rift-valley region between Murat and Aurillac. Because these *planèzes* were so long a battle-ground during the Hundred Years' War, fewer Romanesque churches have survived than usual, and most of the great medieval castles have gone too.

One that has not is Le Sailhans, imposingly perched on a basalt spur above the upper reaches of the Lander. The little tower at the southern end of the *enceinte*, like an uplifted prow, not quite squarely set into the rock, gives the whole place the air of an ossified battleship: the *corps de logis* extending across the grassy 'deck' could be the bridge. There is a square tower at one end and a slim round one at the other, while from behind it peep four more blue-grey tiled pepper-pot towers. To crown this effect of bizarre irrelevance, the southern façade is richly peopled with windows. But the northern side, punctuated by its fat round towers, is practically blind. This is not a crafty defensive arrangement for the place has been several times rebuilt: despite its lofty position it was twice taken and sacked by the English. In the sixteenth century Le Sailhans passed into the hands of the de la Rochefoucauld family, who sold it to Anne Henard, widow of the Chancellor Antoine Dubourg. Her son, Charles, turned to the Protestant faith and because he sheltered refugees during the wars drew down upon the castle an army under St Hérem, governor of the Auvergne. Charles was ill at the time so his wife hid him in the oven for safety when the place was taken, and he had nearly suffocated before they hauled him out. His wife then turned on St Hérem and stabbed him, so it was she who went to prison in St Flour! Two generations later, Le Sailhans passed by marriage into the d'Estaing family, who seem to have had a gift for acquiring castles this way. Effectively, its history was ended.

An amusing story is told of an earlier *Châtelaine*, possibly one of the widows who succeeded to the inheritance — Antoinette d'Amboise or Anne Henard. Hearing a little gossip in the way such gossip does filter through from the kitchen, she called her head cow-man to her: "They tell me you're talking nicely to my chambermaid ..." "That, Madame, is my affair", came the surly reply. "Yes, but if she should 'fill out' as sometimes happens?"

"That, Madame, would be her concern." (Raised eyebrows) — "And the child — who will bring that up?" "Ah! that, Madame, would be your concern!" As Pourrat remarks, the people about here are very independent; but also friendly — they will always give you a wave from their tractor.

Of the villages near Le Sailhans both Roffiac and Andelat have recognisably Romanesque churches: the former has proved a better survivor than the castle whose chapel it once was, of which only a forlorn tower still stands. The architecturally observant will notice that both have niche-apsidal chapels built into the thickness of their walls; Roffiac has some good sculptured capitals with familiar themes — the woman with serpents at her bosom, sirens with tails entwined, and St Michael defeating the dragon, among others. Further north is Coltines, very handsome on its height above a sharply rising main street. Like Andelat it is built of a lovely shade of reddy-brown stone, and the builder has simply adapted his plan to the site by raising the west end higher than the choir. The D.40 from Coltines to Celles offers one of those sudden transformations of landscape which so delight the traveller in the Auvergne; the plateau has been bare and flat and then, as he looks down, all is sylvan and gracious with a stream curling along the narrow valley below wooded heights. In the hollow is Celles, a few houses round a great building, square and rather prison-like, once a 'Commanderie' of the Knights of Malta, now a farm. The pond across the road, the resort of a most exotic gathering of ducks and geese dabbling its greenish, lilied waters when I was there, must surely have been the fish-pond in medieval times?

Out of St Flour the main road south to Rodez, capital of the Aveyron, crosses the Truyère at Lanau and links with the other *grande route*, the N.9, via a lovely upland road from Chaudes-Aigues to St Chély d'Apcher. The lower gorges of the Truyère do not come into our area, the river itself forming the 'frontier' of the Aveyron below Pont de Treboul. But the upper gorges do and they make an admirable excursion, the ruined Château d'Alleuze its focal point.

On the N.121, however, is Les Ternes, a long straggling village pleasantly set on either side of the main highway at a point where three valleys, dipping to the Truyère, meet — hence the origin of its name, 'Ternae valles'. One has to climb, briefly, to look at the château, nicely framed by its wooded garden — a four-storeyed *corps de logis* with crenellation just below the shallow roof and two flat round towers at either end which — unusually — have kept their battlements. The eastern façade has a central tower containing the staircase and a little pepper-pot *tourelle* — as though the big one had pupped — to the left. The present building is of the fifteenth century, for marauding Anglo-Gascon bands had burnt the eleventh-century original. At the time of the rebuilding Les Ternes was owned by the d'Espinchal family. There is a legend — at least, one hopes it is only a legend — that the notorious Gaspard, in a fit of jealous passion, threw his wife's page into one of the caves in the hills nearby and then threw down an ox, not to keep the lad company but to see which would die first! In the eighteenth century the castle passed into the hands of the Rouillon-Spy, notables of St Flour, and it was a Madame Spy des Ternes who sold it to the bishop of St Flour; for sixty years it was the home of a religious order and was then bought by a Monsieur Douhet who again rebuilt it.

In 1972, Les Ternes was evidently unoccupied and the high surrounding walls showed signs of neglect. So I inquired, locally, and was told the previous owner, a lawyer, had married twice and that his second wife, who inherited the place, had fallen out with the children of the previous marriage. Anyway, after the customary legal haggling, the castle was up for sale at £25,000. I have always wanted a smallish château but could not raise the price. Would any reader . . . ?

The gorges of the Truyère, both upper and lower, have been subjected to a series of engineering projects on a grand scale matched only by those on the upper Dordogne. France has always been relatively poor in coal, rich in long, fast-running rivers so the answer to the power-problem was obvious: white coal — *la houille blanche*. Hence the great barrages on the major rivers of the Massif Central. Some people fiercely denounce all this on grounds of environmental change against the course of nature. A case can be made, and when the huge reservoirs (as occasionally happens for engineering reasons) are drained the result is extremely ugly — 'rape of the landscape', indeed. Yet the development was inevitable because highly necessary and when the reservoirs are full, far from being ugly they offer great sweeps of water that rival in grandeur the savage landscape around them. Moreover, in recent years a wise departmental authority has seen that they can be a source of public amenity — as yachting centres, for example. There are schemes already in operation on the barrage de Granval, below the Viaduc de Garabit near St Flour, on the Dordogne just above Bort and at St Etienne-Cantalès on the Cère at the western edge of the Cantal. The dams themselves are monumental structures, to me a trifle frightening in their arrogant restraint of that most terrifying of natural forces, floodwater. But the engineering is sound and the potential vagaries of the climate well-known, so there is little danger. And once the huge concrete walls have been left behind, Nature reasserts itself. Above the Truyère, whose forested gorges are deeper and more spectacular than any except those on the Tarn, one soon forgets them. What remains in the memory is the buzzard, circling tirelessly on wide wings marvellously adapted to take advantage of spiralling currents of air and emphasizing, in his silent power, the uncanny quietness of these high places: on an early summer afternoon the only sounds are the distant murmur of a tractor, the barking of a shepherd-dog, the tinkle of bells on cattle one perhaps cannot see, as they feed on the bush grass of a meadow hidden from view by the wooded bluff immediately below.

The Truyère is also remarkable for having abruptly changed direction. Geologists believe, on the evidence of alluvial deposits that can still be seen near St Flour, that during the relatively recent — pre-historically speaking — upheavals of the tertiary era some fifty million years ago that it once flowed north to join the Alagnon and so, via the Allier, the Loire. Then, when the Pyrenees heaved upwards to cause further folding in the Monts du Cantal, it was forced to turn westward by the raising of the *planèze* and so found a new course through the huge fault that winds down to the Lot, which it now joins at Entraygues. For this we, as travellers, and the French, as devourers of electricity, should be duly grateful.

The ruins of Alleuze can be approached from Villedieu (whose church has a 'miraculous' Virgin) or along the D.40 from St Flour — an upland road offering magnificent views towards the Massif Cantalien and south across la Margeride. Now quite isolated by the waters of the Barrage de Grandval, it was once the vital strategic point commanding the southern approaches to

St Flour. Two of the infamous guerrilla chiefs held the place; Aimérigot le Marché, who killed the rightful owner for insulting his jester, and Bernard Garlain, 'the Wicked Hunchback', who had to be bought out in the end, largely at the expense of the citizens of St Flour. One wonders how they found the money for they were reduced, in the 1380s, to burning their wooden roofs for firewood, so infested was the region by these out-of-work *routiers* who lived by pillage. Little more than a tower and the crumbled remains of the *donjon*, Alleuze is one of the most picturesque sites in the Auvergne; lonely, abandoned, like a half-drowned finger pointing at the sky from its grassy mound. Along the wooded heights on the east side came the Resistance fighters on their way to and from Chaudes-Aigues as the battle ebbed from Mont Mouchet; and the Germans bombed the neighbouring villages, especially Fridefont and Anterrieux, almost to bits.

Chaudes-Aigues, rebuilt after its battering in 1944, has the hottest medicinal waters in the Auvergne and is now a thriving holiday-centre. The Romans had also come here to cure their rheumatism and, no doubt, to make use of the 'natural' central-heating system which the natives have always used and which they adapt to such convenient purposes as cooking and the incubation of eggs. Three-quarters of the houses are 'piped in' to this system through conduits made of pine-wood! The town has a pleasantly busy, preoccupied air and even if you do not have rhematism its situation at the meeting of four roads, with diverse and beautiful country all around, makes it a convenient place to stay. The castle at the top of the hill, on the road to Rodez, is Montvallat. Totally rebuilt in 1610 after a fire, it was surprised in 1585 by a raiding force of Huguenots who carried off the treasure from the church of St Martin and St Blaise at Chaudes-Aigues, which the citizens had thought safe to store there. The little building at the south-west corner — like a truncated tower roofed over — once housed the hunting-dogs: it is now a *pigeonnier*.

From the Rodez road (which winds rather viciously up to the high plateau of the Aveyron) there is a turn left into the D.13; this minor road forks again just before St Rémy de Chaudes-Aigues to keep us within the southward reaching 'beak' of the Cantal towards the point where it joins both the Lozère and the

Aveyron. The object of the journey is the big village of St Urcize — quite the prettiest in this part of the Cantal and remarkable, also, for its church. I came to it from the Nasbinals road, which follows the valley of the little river Bès. From here St Urcize still has the look of the fortified *enceinte* it once was, huddled about the sturdy walls of its church, a last refugee in case of dire assault. The village is all grey stone walls, creepered or gay with rambler roses, sixteenth- and seventeenth-century doorways, and houses with the air of having grown reluctantly out of the Middle Ages (the 'Gendarmerie' has taken over one of the best fifteenth-century buildings). The streets have that friendly medieval habit of leading back into each other after descending a level or two to accommodate the narrow hill-top site.

The church is capped by the typical rectangular bell-tower, called *clocher à peigne*, with which the visitor will be familiar after Roffiac, Andelat and the villages south of St Flour; some of these carry a little roof on either side, presumably to protect the bells from the more violent assaults of the weather; but the one at St Urcize stands defiantly unprotected, with a little cross in the middle above the four round-arched openings. The *chevet* (or apsidal east end) is the only one to survive in the Cantal — tribute perhaps to the remoteness of this place at the confluence of three Departments. It is, apparently, the fruit of an ambitious rebuilding in the late twelfth century; the treatment of the engaged columns of the central 'mass' above the choir is particularly good. The day was overcast when I went there and since the church is rather squat the interior is not well-lit; but I remember an excellent 'Entombment of Christ' in the chapel behind the main altar while the sacristy contains a silver chalice from which the doomed Louis XVI took communion in the prison of the Temple, in Paris.

If you have lunched in St Urcize and wish to spend the afternoon in this wild, open country bordering on the Gévaudan where the famous 'beast' (overgrown wolf or half-man, half-bear, depending on the teller of the tale) once roamed, you may profitaibly trespass into the Lozère as far as the Château de La Baume, just off the D.73 — the shortest route from Chaudes-Aigues to Marvejols. This is a very beautiful castle built of great blocks of grey-brown local stone and crowned by lauze-tiled roofs. At once rustic and grand, La Baume is set on a low rise and half-encircled by a protecting screen of beech and oak trees. Its history, quite the most fascinating I have ever read and well-documented, is far too complex to retail here. But if you can read French, the admirable guide by the Marquis Emmanuel de Las Cases, the present owner, tells the whole intriguing but — humanly speaking — deplorable story with great concision and clarity. Anyone with a penchant for detective fiction with a background of inheritance through twisted legal chicanery will find it impossible to put down. It was the villain of the piece, César de Peyre, called 'Le Grand César' although he was a very short man, who refurnished the place in the style of *Louis Quatorze* during the two decades on either side of the eighteenth century, remodelled the south façade in the long, elegantly balanced manner of Versailles and created the ornate chapel devoted to the cult of St Michael. His portrait hangs in the *grand salon* and if ever a painting accurately reflected the ruthless and avaricious character of its subject this one does. The predominantly Louis XIV interior is extremely beautiful, far more so than that of Parentignat, near Issoire, which is cluttered and inelegant by comparison. Ironically — but how justly if evil-doing is not to achieve any lasting reward — César had no heir, neither son nor daughter; so he left the property to the grandson of his sister, Victoire, the only relative he did not dislike or deliberately offend. His descendants did not value the place so that eventually it came to the Las Cases. Hence the interesting collection of Napoleonic souvenirs, for it was another Emmanuel de las Cases who accompanied the emperor to his exile on St Helena and wrote the best known book on his capitivity, *Le mémorial de Sainte-Hélène*.

A diversion eminently worthwhile across a curiously haunting — and haunted — part of the country. Those who pause at the hamlet of Prinsuejols and look up the hill towards the druidical arrangement of stones on its summit will understand what I mean. Dolmens are by no means rare in this countryside, and the 'beast' — or its ghost — could well prowl there now, so stark and weird is the atmosphere of this rock-strewn plain.

Quite a large, unevenly shaped slice of the country south-west of St Flour and Murat falls into the Department of Aveyron, as do the lower gorges of the Truyère below the 'Belvédère de

Vezou', and the Aveyon falls outside the scope of this book. Let us, therefore, take the broad swathe of hills (whose peak is the Plomb du Cantal, at about 5,000 feet) which dips and climbs, climbs and dips again even more sharply, to the tiny plain watered by the Cère and the Jordanne where stands the lively town of Aurillac at the meeting point of five *grandes routes*.

Murat, some sixteen miles from St Flour, a charming little town hospitable to the visitor and with some good restaurants in the lower quarter, is beautifully set on the south-eastern slopes of a spur of the *Plomb*, with the Alagnon, hastening to an early maturity from its source above Le Lioran, at its feet. The town has a close-set, mildly claustrophobic air; the sort of place, one feels, a man in his maturity might find constricting but to which he would willingly return upon retirement on a modest income. The houses, by no means gloomy, are tall and sober, with the steeply-pitched blue-tiled roofs and elegant *tourelles* characteristic of the towns and villages in the northern half of the Cantal. In the southern parts builders use the russet-orange tile more common on the Lot and middle Dordogne. Truthfully, Murat is more attractive when seen from above the Rocher de Bonnevie, where the seignurial château, destroyed at Richelieu's command, once stood; or from the south-east on the levelled grassy height occupied by the handsome church of Bredons (if one can ignore the mess behind the railway-station). It prospers, now, by the creation of cheese — the word 'manufacture' applied to the delicious varieties of *fromages d'Auvergne* seems inappropriate — and by its sawmills. History relates no violent sackings or reversals of fortune, and the most famous local soldier, the Comte d'Anterroches, fought his battles far away in Germany and the Lowlands in the mid-eighteenth century wars for supremacy in Europe. Before Maastricht, to a despondent fellow-officer who believed their task impossible, he declared with splendid inaccuracy: "That word, Sir, is not in the French language". His castle, a curious but rather pleasing mixture of styles as though the architect were torn between the Classical and the early 'Romantic', stands above the road to Le Lioran. The principal church, Notre-Dame-des-Oliviers, was struck not — for a change — by the English or their Gascon *routiers* but by lightning: which presumably accounts for the modern façade. The 'miraculous' Black Virgin, papally crowned in 1878, is now robed in green brocade and set on high beside a rather hideous Baroque altar, strangely *classé monument*. The interior is wide, spacious and rather impersonal, and marred by an unusual clutter of statuary.

Not so the splendid lauze-tiled, brownstone church of Bredons, which has a remarkably high nave, a massive squat tower and the sharply 'cut-off' treatment of the apse (*chevet plat*) quite often found in the Cantal. As one might expect in a priory-foundation of the mid-eleventh century, isolated in such solitary grandeur on its hill, Bredons was a fortified church though little trace of this original building remains. Its most beautiful feature is the south portal, with triple arches composed of multiple voussoirs. These and the rich billet decoration round the upper arch and above the capitals of the massive pillars, are broadly reminiscent of the doorways of certain churches in Normandy: architecture of sophisticated simplicity. The interior has recently been restored. The work was not complete in 1972 so the church had a rather unlived-in air, accentuated by its great height. There are several good Baroque altars but the sculptured-wood surrounds of the great piers are more interesting; one relief shows St Jerome drawing the thorn from his lion's foot and there are some excellent heads, one of a youth with a long nose and a receding chin, others portraying more military-type faces. Striking, too, is the Crucifixion with three mourning figures below the cross; Mary, well-built and rather Spanish-looking, kneels at her Son's feet. Overall, a fine if rather sombre church: but the site is beautiful — well worth the short detour.

The road up to the Plomb, through Albepierre, is delightfully pretty and offers one enchanting glimpse of that village as it climbs towards the Prat du Bouc. Here, because of the height, trees are sparse and there are magnificent views a little further on, looking east. From this aspect the Plomb — the highest point in the Cantal — modulates upwards in a series of gentle, breast-like rises. The last time I was there snow was still lying in early June and on a stormy, sultry day, masses of grey-white cloud driven by a rain-bearing wind from the south-west threw dark pools of shadow along the scree-strewn slopes. Several cows were picturesquely outlined, motionless, on a ridge; while in the open space beneath the Prat du Bouc, where a *buvette* was in process of building, goats sheltered from the heat beneath an articulated lorry. One does see goats in these wild parts and — occasionally — oxen drawing a plough or cart. All over the Cantal the cow is queen. Quite rightly, she does not disturb her leisured, dignified gait to convenience the passing car, while the cowherds clearly expect her to be given priority. One lady poked her muzzle through my open side-window blew gently through her moist notrils and withdrew as if mildly shocked to find another animate being confined in a tin box. Personally I never wished to hurry these beasts. Long-legged and elegant, whether of the velvet fawn or the *frisé* chestnut-red Salers breed, they are seldom mired or caked with mud; and their progress is most musical.

The churches in this area are usually of the late fourteenth or fifteenth century, with massive cross vaulting, while most (Pierrefort is a notable exception) have the trim *clocher à peigne*. Valuejols — a pleasant, sleepy village — has a finely restored interior with a good Crucifixion on the north wall and, most unusually, a stone-pulpit with carvings of Christ and the evangelists. The big church at Paulhac, also rebuilt after the Hundred Years' War, has another fine Christ; but I remember this village for its lovely situation and the little *manoir*, thick-walled and snug, set contentedly above its garden like an old warrior gone to ground. Not far up the road towards the Plomb is another domesticated old soldier, the Château de Belinay, at the foot of a steep narrow lane, with a dainty *tourelle* at one corner and a fatter one tucked into the angle of its walls where the medieval part joins on to the later *corps de logis*. All round here there are superb views from the excellent minor-roads branching down to the N.121: the shoulders of the Plomb block the distant prospect of the Puy Mary and its neighbouring peaks, but on a clear day one can see twenty or thirty miles, north-west to le Limon above Dienne, and to the Puy de la Gravière: and north-east to the wooded Suc Grand below Allanche and Vernols, where the knight from the Holy Land found the dying hermit and left a wolf to guard him.

Further south the only large market-town is Pierrefort, a proud place, very up-and-down and roundabout, with a nineteenth-century château primly perched on a pinnacle of rock above the Vezou and what must be just about the tallest spire in the Cantal to crown its modern church. Pierrefort has always had the reputation of being a tough, unviolated town. In the *parlement*

of St Flour they used to call out 'Apchon-Pierrefort' and
then — immediately — 'Pierrefort-Apchon' so as not to offend
anyone's susceptibilities, although Apchon was the senior
barony.

The road to Brezons crosses one of the highest parts of the
plateau. This is sparsely inhabited country for between the
curiously named Forêt de Ciniq, on the slopes of the Puy
Francio, and the Pas de Cère, which overlooks Vic and the
valley-road winding down to Aurillac, there are no villages at
all. Occasionally — locked as it were, into these upland
fastnesses — one loses all sense of time; freed of the constant
pressures of urban life, some apparently irrelevant incident
remains printed on the memory like a still from a motion-picture.
The day I went to Brezons I noticed a car parked well off the
road in the undergrowth, looked about for the owner and saw,
in the middle distance, a herdsman waving frantically (I could
just hear him yell) at a group of impassive cows champing on the
ridge, their fawn coats a vivid contrast against the old-gold of the
broom, still in flower after a tardy spring. There was a murmur
of bees and the pungent scent of herbs after a shower of
rain — no sense of time at all.

The herdsman was still gesticulating wildly as I drove on. Two
alarmingly sharp bends (the road teeters over a sheer drop to the
valley, hundreds of feet below) and Brezons came in sight, a
baker's dozen of houses round a squat Romanesque church. The
columns of the nave are of a most strangely-textured stone,
speckled black and red on grainy grey. But the best feature of this
church is the 'transitional' doorway, with griffons' heads and
luxuriant foliage cushioning the tops of the engaged colonnettes.
Lower down the street was a café-restaurant, cavernous and bare
inside; the woman who served me stared, and a young farmer on
a tractor outside replied mechanically to my greeting as if in a
dream. Few strangers arrive here before August; perhaps they
thought high summer come upon them unawares. However,
further up the valley-road, over the bridge, a farmer and his
handsome son, scythes in hand, talked very civilly of the *deuxième
coupe* — the second cut of hay they were about to make in their
meadows — and showed me where the castle was. So I
continued up the valley to where the challenging, rather
Provençal towers of La Boyle may just be seen, high among the

trees to the right. Little more than a rectangular *donjon* but well over 100 feet high, with elegant machicoulis extending the length of its walls, this must have been a fearsomely difficult place to take: Richelieu evidently thought so for, in 1628, he had the outer walls and postern demolished. With their stone the defensive ditches were filled in and the terraces, on three levels, built up in order (as the little guide to the Cantal castles remarks) ". . . to soften the severity of a building which, within the rules of a military architecture, is a masterpeice of logic and efficiency". La Boyle was owned ɔy the family of Brezons, renowned soldiers. Most of this family were proud knights, loyal to their king and Church. One of them, however, fell so low as to have his young brother murdered by hired assassins. No-one reproached him for the crime (though a plaque in the village where it was committed still does). But retribution followed in the shape of a neighbour, Renaud de Murat, whom Pierre Brezons had offended by taking the other side in a quarrel. Renaud arrived unexpectedly one evening, took the castle and burnt it, a contemporary chronicler noting that the Brezons serfs and retainers "grilled like chickens" inside. The owner, taken prisoner, had to watch his castle burn and, for good measure, to pay a large ransome for his liberty. It was this Pierre who built La Boyle in its present form to replace his other gutted castle.

A later owner, Charles, was such a fervent supporter of the ultra-Catholic 'League' during the Religious Wars that he became known as the scourge of the Protestants (he was largely responsible for the massacre of the reformists of Aurillac). Eventually, the Protestants had their revenge for they took the castle and ravaged the surrounding villages. As usual, it was the peasantry who suffered for the excesses of their betters.

In the late eighteenth century the Brezons line died out and the Revolution allowed a local farmer to set up in their stead. As recently as 1960 the present owner, formerly Mayor of Nancy, found La Boyle and set about restoring it.

Further south — trespassing just a little over the Aveyron border — are tiny villages of such untouched solitude and quietness one almost tiptoes through them: one of these, Nigressière, has a white dove above a painted zodiac on its church-tower, while on a primitive graveyard-cross the Christ figure stares out of huge blank eyes, their sockets whitened and eroded by rain and wind. Sinhalac appears quite deserted — and possibly is. Yet Thérondels, a larger village with a grand and well-kept church, has a *Logis-de-France* hotel and so has Paulherols on the D.54. This is a place of rare charm. Just outside it one comes, suddenly, to what must surely be one of the great views of the Cantal, looking right down the Cère valley and far beyond to the high ridges the other side of Aurillac and the purple-blue hills of the 'chestnut country' above the Lot valley. Distances are magical in the southern Cantal, seldom crystal clear in high summer but always subtly changing in colour as great fleets of cloud drift across the sky to shadow and soften the landscape.

Needless to say, as one leaves the high, bare plateau and drops down to the bosky fertility of the Cère valley, the country blossoms into a florescence of châteaux of the more civilised kind. A bend in the main road from Mur-de-Barrèz to Raulhac reveals that of Messilhac proudly set on a ledge in the valley against a background of trees, quite enfolded by them on three sides, in fact, so that one only comes to it down a narrow, rutted lane loomed over by huge chestnuts and elms. The fine Renaissance doorway is crowned by the head and blazon of its builder, Jean de Montamat. But scarcely has the visitor passed inside than he reads — on the face of it — an odd sort of welcome:

> Who comes in here and nothing brings
> Be well advised to pass the door
> For our condition cannot allow
> Inside (who) comes with empty hands.

Indeed, one *is* reluctant to pass inside but only because the view is so superb. The guide, I regret to say — a Gascon by his accent — has something in common with this welcome in that he tells you little, and that offhandedly, but obviously expects much in return. The apartments should not retain anyone from a good lunch except that, at the very end of the visit, the columbarium in the western tower is a magnificent example of the master-carpenter's art — a great wheel of roof timbers in mint condition, which astonishes by its ordered complexity.

The last of the Montamat line took as her final husband — she had three — Raymond Chapt de Rastinhac, a distinguished gentleman who became Lieutenant-General of the Haute-Auvergne: "War, diplomacy, finance, Catholic League, Huguenots . . .". The list is endless. He must have been a hugely energetic man. Sad to say he met a violent end, killed in the cold northland, by the Oise, besieging a castle. His descendants, however, kept Messilhac until 1766.

Below Raulhac — a handsome village whose farm-houses look like manors, and dowered with views Monsieur de Rastinhac himself might have envied — is a rather despondent building, obviously a farm, but with a pretty staircase leading up to a balustraded terrace — the former 'Château de Cropières'. Across what must have been the garden trickles a rivulet dibbled in by dusty hens; the walls surrounding this courtyard are unkempt though the house, if desolate, seems in sound repair. Difficult, however, to imagine this the home of pretty, blonde Marie-Angélique de Scorailles, Duchesse de Fontanges 'maîtresse en titre' to Louis XIV: she was born here but died at the austere convent of Port-Royal, already out of favour and supposedly of a miscarraige. "Beautiful as an angel, empty as a basket", she had (according to Mme. de Sévigné) "as little spirit as a kitten". A Cantalienne innocent abroad, perhaps, in a Court of vicious intrigue and wolfish morals. Yet she was reputed kindly and passed on most of the Sun-King's gifts to her family in the Auvergne.

Originally a medieval fortress belonging to the Monjou family, Cropières was sacked by the English, rebuilt in the sixteenth century and then 'developed', presumably with Marie-Angélique's money, in 1681 and 1720 into something resembling its present state, though the west wing has now disappeared. A bust of the young Louis XIV in the centre of the façade and the armorial shields of the Fontanges and the Scorailles at either end seem only to mock the little castle's elegant past. *Plus ça change, plus ça changera* . . .

If Cropières is saddening, Jou-sous-Monjou, from which the ancient barony took its name, is both pretty and weird. Worth visiting, certainly, for the Romanesque church, a rustic gem. Notice the curious, primitive heads and decorations all round the doorway, while the corbel-heads on the south side of the nave are a most bizarre collection — early versions of familiar Auvergnat themes: the man with his chin in his hands, two birds drinking from the same bowl, the gaunt horse-face often found in churches on the plateau. A pity an ugly hut behind the apse so spoils the total effect of this truly 'country' Romanesque.

In contrast, the little town of Vic-sur-Cère, reached by an extremely pretty road over the Col de Curebourse, seems positively sophisticated. The town's gay and holiday-air matches its beginning for the abbey-church about which it grew was founded by one Pierre, troubadour by nature, monk by ill-chosen vocation, who made of it in the mid-twelfth century an oasis of culture, only to go travelling to the courts of Philippe-Auguste and our own Richard Coeur-de-Lion. He must have been a good musician for he won prizes at many of the festivals of his time, including the 'golden falcon' at Le Puy. Vic was sacked by the men of Falgoux under the Sieur d'Apchon, the most infamous robber-baron of these parts, while a ravine nearby was the scene of one of Merle's more engaging exploits. Ambushed by a troop of Catholics while convoying supplies for the Protestant armies up-country, he found himself outnumbered. So he had the traces of his mule-teams cut and beat a hasty retreat, only to halt when out of sight. Presently, he regrouped his men and quietly returned to the place: his stratagem had worked for the Catholics, having stopped to sample his supplies, were already muzzy with wine. He lost no time in cutting them to pieces.

The old town is full of good houses with the trim gardens that help to give most *bourgades* in this part of the Cantal the air of being urban extensions of the surrounding country. Down the hill towards the river there are public gardens, avenues of trees, playgrounds for the children, and the river itself has been made suitable for boating. The hotels are good but unpretentious, the tourist facilities well-organised; the place is admirably situated to make the best of its natural attractions. Need one say more?

The main road from Murat to Aurillac, through Vic-sur-Cère, is one of the most beautiful in the Cantal, rivalled only by the D.17 along the next valley to the west followed by the river Jordanne; and by the 'Route des Crètes', perhaps the most beautiful of all since it offers magnificent views across the Cirque de Mandailles, towards the Plomb and its adjoining peaks, and to those 'building up' to the Puy Mary, whose grey dome almost matches the Plomb for height. These two form as it were, the

Saugues; church tower

Auvergnat country house refurnished in the traditional style

St Flour; upper town seen from the Lander

Château de Saillant near St Flour

Vallée de la Truyère and the Château d'Alleuze

Musicians in traditional costume

Maurs; portal of church, fifteenth century

Salers; Grande Place

Mauriac; the old quarter

Château de Val on the reservoir near Bort

knobbly boned 'wrist' from which the ridges splay like fingers down to the plain where the Jordanne joins the Cère. And since this geological formation determines the communications-network, Aurillac has developed of recent years into the liveliest and most outward-looking township in the Auvergne, apart from Clermont itself.

Thiézac, the only large village between Vic and Murat, is famous for the aptly named *Notre Dame de la Consolation* on a *butte* to the north. To this chapel came Anne of Austria, Louis XIII's much-troubled queen. Caught up in the dynastic conflicts between the royal houses of France and Spain, her ladies-in-waiting the pawns of Richelieu in his attempts to gain dominance over the emotionally wayward king, Anne had one overwhelming desire — to have a child. So her visit, ostensibly to take the waters at Vic was probably to pray at the shrine of the Virgin here, for the Lady was reputed to take pity on women in her situation. Anyway, she did have a child after twenty-two years of sterile marriage — the future Louis XIV. The chapel, ornately decorated inside, is finely placed — a site of quiet, arboreal charm even now as in the seventeenth century, and the village — once off the main road — has the same restful quality.

This is grand walking country. One must, in fact, walk for there are virtually no roads suitable for cars above Thiézac. Le Lioran, some ten miles on towards Murat, has been developed as a winter-sporting centre, but its hotels, rather more sophisticated than those elsewhere, are equally popular with summer visitors and the ambiance has not been spoilt by the new roads built to accommodate the winter traffic. From here, there are paths by which one may gain the western slopes of the *Plomb* and, on the other side of the road, the arrogant height of the Puy de Bataillouse.

South of Vic, as the valley widens, is pre-eminently château country. Comblat, on the outskirts of the town, was the home of th de Lacarrière family, "people of justice that came from the soul", Henri Pourrat assures us. They were distinguished administrators in the Cantal, the last of them also a noted astronomer. His daughter handed over the castle to the *Département*, which has turned it into an Agricultural College for women. May their cheeses prosper! The façade, which has dignity rather than charm, owes its seventeenth-century style to — did you guess? having been ruined by the English during the Hundred Years' War.

Pesteils, down the road, has both dignity and charm. Its tall *donjon*, shallow-roofed and chimneyed, is a landmark for miles around, and the rest of it, a happily informal arrangement of small towers and mansards about the steeply pitched roof of its eighteenth-century 'corps de logis', nestles comfortably into the lushly-wooded background. It can be visited; the young guide, when I was there, proved courteously informative. The medieval castle was almost completely rebuilt in the eighteenth and nineteenth centuries for it, too, was ravaged by the English and the Huguenots, while the Revolutionaries did not treat it kindly either. (The Comte de Miramon and his wife had chosen to go into exile and this usually provoked the local 'enragés' to wanton destruction). However, the family was given leave to return in 1794 and their letters of safe-conduct are on display. Other letters testify the family's good service to three kings of diverse politics; Henri III, Henri IV, and Louis XIII. The tower, whose six storeys are served by a staircase built into the walls, was begun as a les Foulholes of the family that founded the medieval castle, and finished by one of the Montamat, who originally owned Messilhac; their family emblem, a prancing lion, can be seen in the last room, while the arms of both families are joined over the doorway of the central tower. The interior of Pesteils is full of interest: the painted ceilings of the first floor rooms are excellent seventeenth-century work, representing the prowess of the de Miramon family and the fall of Icarus; a warning, perhaps, against undue arrogance. In the central tower are other interesting frescoes of the fifteenth century showing the instruction of a noble youth by his tutor and feats of chivalry by four heroes who might have served as his models.

As at La Boyle, the *emplacements* of the outer medieval walls have served to form terraces for the gardens: the view from these terraces, gently beautiful, offers a glimpse of two smaller castles, Clavières and Vixouse, on the first wooded ridge beyond the Cère. The latter, very weathered and rustic now, has had some intersting proprietors. One of the Brunenc family that held it during the first half-century of our millennium was a troubadour who became a monk out of thwarted love. Anther, François-Xavier Pagès, founded and financed the first local newspaper in this region.

One can, in fact, take the pretty by-road out of the valley through Vixouze to Badailhac in order to reach Carlat. Here, on the huge table of basalt rock above a handful of houses, existed the most famous castle of the Cantal, the key-fortress guarding the western approaches to the Haute-Auvergne long before the road up the Cère valley became the main highway. Its extent can be gauged from the fact that the village itself once sheltered behind its outer walls, and it is a good fifteen minutes' climb up to the rock-shelf on which the castle itself stood, with so many towers that each had a name — Tour Noire, Tour Guillot, Tour Margot, Tour St Jean, and so on. One of the best *baillis* who ever governed this region, Eustache de Beaumarchais, held it for St Louis; but the English stormed it in 1369 and Bernard Garlan, 'Le Méchant Bossu', took it over when bought out of Alleuze. He had to be bought out of Carlat, too. By the mid-fifteenth century, in the reign of Louis XI, 'the universal spider', it had come into the possession of Jacques d'Armagnac of the Gascon family whose quarrels with the Burgundian dukes had made it relatively easy for the British to keep their hold over a kingdom racked by its own quarrelling nobles. Jacques, however, was no brutal medieval baron, more the soldier-courtier type of Renaissance Italy — charming, suave, political in the worst sense. A friend of Louis's rebellious youth, he overplayed his hand at last; pinned into Carlat by a huge royal army, he surrendered after an eighteen-month siege. Louis had already pardoned him twice for his treacheries; this time he was taken to Paris, strung up in a cage above the street for all to see, 'examined' by a commission determined to winkle out his allies and beheaded in Les Halles. This marked the end of those great 'Princes of the Blood' who had so impoverished the Auvergne. Henceforth no royal prince would be allowed enough power to make the province a part of his own little kingdom.

Carlat was not, however, dismantled by Richelieu; Henri IV had already done the job for him in order to deny it to the Catholic extremists of the League. Before this it had been taken by the Protestants in 1568. Later, La Reine Margot was brought to Carlat, at Henri's command, to keep her out of mischief. Here, too, she fell in love with d'Aubiac, who was to be judicially murdered at Usson. No doubt, she would have preferred Carlat to that hemmed-in, windy place. For even then the 'Carladez' must have been a gracious, relatively civilised country, with the craftsmen and merchants of Aurillac within easy reach and fertile farms from which to draw supplies.

Now Carlat is only a flat, grassy table of land, artificially breached and grazed over by sheep. One can climb to it from the upper village and re-people the site in one's mind. The view is superb. Queen Margot's 'staircase' in the rock is still there to come down by, and an inscription in the church below (which has a fine Baroque altar in polychrome wood) records the destruction of the fortress. One eats excellently in the little hotel on the main road.

Returning to Aurillac one summer afternoon, I turned right at Vézac and found, just off the D.108, beneath a thickly wooded bluff whose trees extend their shelter right across the road, the lovely, rustic old manor of Caillac. Leaving the car on the verge, I was met by two piglets trotting briskly in the opposite direction. Since there is quite a lot of traffic and they were hardly of an age for slaughter we had a short chase before they were persuaded back into the farmyard that now occupies the forecourt. The manor has a jumble of balconies with wooden balustrades, mansards like brows over the sunken eyes of old men and lauze-tiled roofs licheny with time. A delightful place of no history at all that I could discover. If Falstaff had been French, he would have had a country cousin here, red wine to drink, and money for the borrowing.

"The holy Count Géraud who possessed immense lands in the Haute-Auvergne", writes a modern historian, "founded the abbey of Aurillac in 894, endowing it richly. Its lands . . . made this monastery one of the richest in France but to its reputation for wealth it soon added one for intellectual pursuits." To this centre of early medieval culture came Gerbert, a boy of great gifts. These he developed by going to Spain to study the mathematical science of the Moors and, later, to Reims, at that time the foremost centre of religious learning in Europe. Not only a thinker but a practical scientist, he popularised the use of the abacus for counting, made a pendulum clock and somehow contrived an organ that worked by steam. Very late in life, after helping to create the Christian kingdoms of Poland and Hungary, he became the first French pope, Sylvester II. Between them, military saint and pope created the beginnings of Aurillac, around the great abbey on the banks of the Jordanne. (Later there was constant friction between abbey and town authority as the merchant 'consuls' tried to take over its government). Except during the latter part of the sixteenth and the early seventeenth centuries, the little city grew more and more prosperous: during the later Middle Ages its merchants, together with those of St Flour, sold their textiles and hides as far afield as Spain and in the Champagne where they had special marketing facilities allotted to them.

Aurillac is still a commercial place even if — so far as I know — no-one now trawls the Jordanne with a fleece in the hope of dredging up gold-dust. The town is currently well-known for making umbrellas and furniture, activities which the practical Gerbert would no doubt have approved. Visually, however, the visitor might find it hard to credit the medieval affluence because — in reprisal for the execution of some eighty Protestants in 1551 — the Huguenot leader, des Adrets, took and burnt Aurillac eight years later after laying waste the outlying monasteries and killing the monks. Colbert revived it about 100 years later by encouraging the manufacture of lace and establishing new tanneries. The so-called 'Maison Consulaire' is the only sixteenth-century house of any note to have survived: the Palais de Justice, with a row of medallion-heads high on the façade, is a good example of bad restoration, but the abbey-church of St Géraud, basically Gothic, has very recently been restored in excellent taste. And the little *place* it occupies has a quaint old fountain in dark marble.

Here, in 1972 when Aurillac was celebrating its millennary, they danced the *bourrée* to the music of the Auvergnat bagpipes and the squeaky, stringed *vielles*. This dance, for which the Auvergne is known all over France thanks to the innumerable *émigrés* in Paris and elsewhere who launch into it on festive occasions, is not spectacular in the Spanish style. Rather, I would say, it typifies the dignified reticence, even in enjoyment, of this mountain-people who remain so attached to their cultural traditions. The men, dressed predominantly in black short jackets, tight trousers and wide-crowned hats, the women in dark skirts with white blouses set off by lace decoration or coloured shawls, skip neatly and demurely to rather stilted rhythms — dictated, probably, by the heavy sabots that were commonly worn until the twentieth century. *Michelin Vert* is a trifle condescending about all this; for there has been something of a revival of folkdancing in the smaller towns and not only for the benefit of the tourist. I, personally, enjoyed the *bourée*, as the people themselves evidently do. Music and dancing rather than literature is their cultural heritage; the musical life in Clermont, during the winter, is quite rich for a provincial city and there is a very reasonable symphony orchestra.

Aurillac certainly made the most of its celebrations in 1972. In the huge castle at the top of the hill leading up from the Boulevard des Hortes (a modern reconstruction except for the eleventh-century *donjon*), there was a magnificent exhibition, using papiermâché models, natural materials and photographic montage, of the geology of the Haute-Auvergne with great attention paid to the volcanic origins of the mountains, as well as some excellent documentation on the Romanesque sculpture in the churches. Of this, oddly enough, there is practically nothing in the town. Evidently, what churches there were of this period des Adrets destroyed. But Notre-Dame des Neiges, formerly a Franciscan monastery — situated just off the pretty main square, whose centre is all garden — is worth visiting for the gothic sacristy and the fine fifteenth-century chapel leading off it. Apart from the abbey-church, which is still rather new and 'hard' after the thorough restoration, it is easily the best church in Aurillac.

The old quarter along the river on the northern edge of the town has retained some of its atmosphere. Across the narrow bridge the D.17 follows the Jordanne valley closely; and if the road branching off it is aptly named 'the route over the crests', this one should be called *la route des châteaux* for there seems to be one every kilometre until the road begins to climb steeply after Velzic: all are small and private, the prettiest the curiously named Château d'Oyez near Belliac, of browny-red stone and tucked into itself as if frightened of visitors. St Simon is a charming hamlet: turn right past the nice-looking hotel, cross the bridge and you come to a little square quite dominated by a huge, riven elm — the two parts cemented together to make it safe for children to climb — and by a tower dissociated from the church. Inside which, pulling aside a red curtain, I found Queen Victoria, bun and all, presiding over what looks like a double-bed that contains no visible evidence of "dearest Albert". Some day I must go back and find out who this stern lady really is.

Mandailles has the best church along this road; two faces half-human, half-demon glare at you from the corbels over the portal. Inside, there is a sumptuously carved pulpit, some elegant foliage and animal capitals and fascinating misericords under the choir-stalls; one figure with a pair of goat's horns growing out of his temples, another plucking at his forked beard (the hands are always used decoratively), a third with hair — or is it a heavy, straight-edged cap? — completely covering the eyes of a young man's fresh, sensual face. Having come so far as Mandailles, the traveller is committed to the steep climb up to the Puy Mary. Perhaps the most precipitous road in the Auvergne, it rounds the gaunt amphitheatrical scarp known as the 'Cirque de Mandailles' in a series of hair-pin bends, with the bald pate of the Puy Griou up-right and the Puy Chavaroche, almost as high as 'Mary' herself, towering over the Col de Redonder. From here one has superb views down the forested slopes of the Cirque de Falgoux, the rock-wall complementing that of Mandailles and overlooking the neck of the valley of the same name. From the Puy Mary, the best views are north across the next range, smoother and gentler in outline and pre-eminently cattle country, for the soil is too thin on these slopes for arable farming; and north-east down the Impradine valley towards Dienne and the even higher, bleaker land above Ségur.

Alternatively, by turning off the D.17 at St Cirgues one can return by the 'Route des Crètes', so called not because it runs along the crests but because it offers such splendid views of the Puy Mary and the Plomb, with their satellite peaks — again, wonderful walking country, with sufficient shade on a hot day in which to rest and admire the views.

Before exploring the upland country on either side of the N.122 (the main traffic artery from Aurillac towards Bort-les-Orgues and the Limousin) no-one should miss the southernmost triangle of the Cantal whose base is the Lot valley; this is the 'chestnut country' already mentioned, thickly wooded, by no means well-populated but rich in interest.

Michelin Vert rather inplies this is infertile country. I did not find it so. The small towns seem prosperous, wheat is now being grown on some of the upland farms, and what villages there are have a solid and well-kept look about them. Tourism has undoubtedly helped: nearly every village I passed through boasted at least one hotel, while both Montsalvy and Maurs obviously set out to cater for the visitor.

Leaving Aurillac by the Figeac road one may soon turn off it to Roannes St Mary and come, by a very pretty road, to Marcolès. This fortified town has kept its medieval air to a quite remarkable extent, thanks to its concentric steet plan and the fact that scarcely a house is under 400 years old. Usually in such places, the church is situated in the inner 'ring' to serve as a last refuge should the outer walls be breached. The one at Marcolès is powerfully built, although it was restored in the sixteenth century — perhaps after a sacking, for the English occupied these parts in force. The interior is impressive in scale but contains little of interest save for a black bust of St Martin and some sculptured figures of the kind found at Salers, in the 'Entombment of Christ' there. Marcolès might be a thought gloomy in poor weather but it is most 'atmospheric' to walk around.

The local château whose grounds border the village cannot be seen until one descends the hill on the D.66. Then, from a bend in the road, there is an enchanting glimpse, up left, of shallow-pitched, lauze-tiled roofs, their mansards shuttered against the sun, and deep fawn walls, with a great barn nearby like a sturdy retainer. The country rolls west in a wide amphitheatrical sweep, dotted with farms with similar long stone barns, the schist in their walls glinting silvery in the mellow light. And on the next rounded hill is the little castle of Fargues where, as I passed one Sunday, a riot of children milled noisily about the lawns, their bright summer clothes restless patches of colour against the brown stone of its walls. Like many châteaux in the Auvergne this one is rented out, in July, as a *colonie de vacances*. How pleasant this must be for town-children cooped up all winter and spring by long French school-hours.

From Marcolès I went down to Calvinet, certainly the prettiest village in this part of the world and nicely situated for exploring the *Chatîgnerie* (there are two good hotels, one a 'Logis de France'). The countryside, richly verdant even for the Cantal, is close-set, with an air of privacy about it as if on guard against any intrusion upon its everyday occasions. The manors, mostly farms, are only seen, secluded behind a copse or screened by a tall avenue of beech or chestnut, as one looks back before descending into the next valley to cross the inevitable stream that freshens its meadows. I would hesitate to describe *La Chataîgnerie* as 'haunted' like the Forez or the Livradois, for it does not have their wide-flung grandeur which so enfolds the travellers into its silences; this is a land to which some handsome prince, done with adventure, might retire to cosset his hard-won princess and bring up a family.

Calvinet is briskly business-like rather than sleepy for it evidently serves the neighbouring farms as market and machine-servicing centre. The steep main street leads into a wide square — meeting-place for the young and their necessary conversations and for older men to play at *boule* before the evening meal. The little hotel on the corner has a flowery terrace overlooking this square and raised above it to a decent level. What more pleasant than to linger over an apéritif and watch the amiable to-and-fro of country-life? There can be few more amiable places in the Cantal than Calvinet, whose *Dame*, in the thirteenth century, married Eustache de Beaumarchais, Military Governor of the Auvergne Mountains for St Louis and a very successful soldier; he tamed even the haughty Sieur d'Apchon, in his plateau fastness 3,000 feet up on the windy borders of the Cézallier.

This was a time of relative quiet and prosperity during the governorship of Alphouse de Poitiers, the king's brother, who ruled the Auvergne far more successfully from Paris than the duc de Berri from his sumptuous castle-palaces at Nonette and Riom. It was de Beaumarchais too who arbitrated between the citizens of Aurillac and their abbot-count when they fell out — not for the first time — over the terms of the Royal Charters, known as *Alfonsines*. Such charters enabled the king to borrow money from prosperous merchants ready to pay for extended trading privileges; a similar franchise was granted to Montsalvy in 1270. Whether Eustache ever lived at the Château de Lamothe down the road from Calvinet is uncertain; probably, he never had time to live anywhere for very long. Of the original fortress nothing remains but the *tour-escalier*; eighteenth- and nineteenth-century rebuildings have left Lamothe very trim and picturesque, even a trifle *nouveau-riche* for this neighbourhood.

Rather more typical is Senézergues, now little more than a 'donjon' with three potent pepperpot towers and another, at the side, which has lost its 'cap'. Beautifully set on a rise above a wooded gorge it was evidently much bigger in the mid-fifteenth century when Archambaut de la Roque obtained permission to build a castle "with towers, crenellations, drawbridge, moat and curtain-walls". De Beaumarchais shared the tenure of this place with another Archambaut, possibly to keep him in order. A later de la Roque was killed beside Montcalm on the heights above Quebec, and the castle was largely dismantled in 1793. One of the places that make me wish I had a few thousand a year to spend on it as a summer *plaisance*.

Montsalvy also has a military past: the Duke of Lancaster — Shakespeare's John of Gaunt — arrived here in 1373, his resources exhausted and with only 3,000 out of the 30,000 men he started out with from Calais. Presumably he was making for Carlat or St Flour. Nothing more peaceful and domestically arranged than Montsalvy now. Unlike Maurs, its counterpart on the western side of the *Chataîgnerie*, the life here is inside the perimeter of the old *enceinte* along one long main street gently sloping from north to south gate, with lanes branching off on either side. The shops are spotlessly clean, the hotels distinctly inviting. The big gateways at either end of the main street help to maintain the town's medieval character, but it is altogether more alive than Marcolès. The little château by the south gate has been patched but not re-vamped and there are lovely old houses in the lanes beyond the square which opens out this southern quarter. The church is handsome but contains little of interest except a well-preserved   and   very   handsome   fifteenth-century 'Crucifixion', the apse being all that remains of the original eleventh-century building, a dependency of the abbey at Aurillac. I doubt if John of Gaunt found Montsalvy as restful and charming as I did — Calais is a long way to come on horseback, fighting all the way. The people, now, are very hospitable and the food is excellent.

North of the town the Puy de l'Arbre, at 2,500 feet, offers grandiose views over these hills and the savage gorges of the Truyère lower to the east. Near Ladinhac, the village below this height, was the castle of Mont-Lauzy, owned by the de Lusignan family of crusading fame. In 1652 the châtelaine, Olympe, was brutally murdered by masked men while her husband was away fighting for the king in Guyenne. The crime seemed pointless, quite without motive. But the *bailli*, a La Carrière from Comblat, near Vic, proved a fine detective; questioning the servants he found out that one of the murderers was left-handed and that the weapon used was a hunting-knife belonging to the castle armoury. Putting two and two together, he looked up his dossier, found that one of the Lusignan servants, a left-handed man, had a criminal record and so brought the lady's murderer to book.

From Calvinet one may drop down to the Lot gorge by the main road, leaving Cassaniouze — another pleasant holiday-village — on the left and the ruins of Riquemaure castle off to the right. An even grander road is the D.119, winding precipitously above the forested gorge of the little river Auze; this one offers superb views, as does the D.41, through Aubespeyre, which joins the Lot valley at Vieillevie. Tucked into a hollow in the cliffs where the river makes a sharp bend, this village is dominated by a large château with handsome fifteenth-century windows. It is apparently uninhabited excepted by swallows which find its crenellated eaves an ideal barrack. It may be visited if one applies to the presbytery. The little white Romanesque church is immaculately kept; inside, the visitor is greeted by two remarkably 'live' busts of St Sebastian and St John Baptist, the former with a sensitive, slightly petulant artist's face. Above the Baroque altar, carved with unusual delicacy, the usual Deity gazes down, spreading out his hands as if to restrain some determined offender from treading the primrose path. But he looks apprehensive too — afraid he will tumble from his curling grey-stucco clouds, perhaps. This is a delightful spot, weathered grey chateau, white stucco church and stone houses making a picturesque ensemble. I took an early *vin blanc* in the bank-side cafe past whose terrace the Lot rushes only a few feet away.

Entraygues, with its magnificent embrasured bridge, lies a few miles up-river over the Aveyron border; while down-stream, over the Pont de Coursavy, a pretty road follows the Dourdou before climbing to Conques, surely the greatest Romanesque monastery-church in south-west France. But the Cantal border twists sharply northwards, here, into the woods above the gorge and one has to return almost to Cassaniouze in order to take the D.25 (the 'border' road) to St Constant. Between Fournoulès and St Constant, on a wooded bluff and so thickly surrounded by

trees it can scarcely be seen, stand the ruins of the Château de
Chaules, one of the Merle family-strongholds. To reach it, take
the lane to the left by the bridge where the Ressegue joins the
infant Célé, and cross the field overlooking the duckpond. At its
edge a path struggles through the undergrowth and traces of the
lower curtain-walls can be seen. Only a *donjon* and a narrow
round tower remain of what must have been an extensive
fortess. Crumbling, laced by creepers and peopled by flowering
shrubs, mysteriously forlorn as only abandoned woodland places
are, Chaules is an ironic monument to the most ingenious
guerilla-warrior of his time.

At Montmurat, further west, prehistoric remains of the kind
frequently found in the Lot valley have been recovered, and
there was once a castle here with thirteen proud towers. Only the
dungeons remain. Maurs, however, is splendidly intact and
thoroughly alive — a fortified town built on a concentric plan
with a double line of plane-trees along the boulevard where the
walls formerly stood. Here all the life of the place flows, that
perennial pattern of shop-counter gossip and café-meeting dear
to such places. Within the medieval *enceinte*, russet-tiled houses
and balconies decked out with geraniums contribute to the
meridional air which distinguishes Maurs from Montsalvy,
whose cool grey stone resembles that of certain 'bastide' towns in
Périgord. The church, built in the fourteenth century, has a fine
main door; it contains a reliquary bust — in this case of St
Césaire, martyred bishop of Arles — similar to that at St
Nectaire. Gilded copper over wood, it has an idol-like quality;
the eyes are powerful, the beard curiously 'live', and one notices
that lengthening of the fingers typical of the holy statues all over
the Auvergne.

In Maurs, on the D.13, a sign directs the traveller to the
Château de l'Estrade. This proves almost invisible behind its
protective copse, but on the hill out of the town there is a
delightful example of the Cantalien manor or *gentilhommière*, the
kind of residence that often belongs to a proprietor who farms his
own land or to a professional man who has made enough money
to retire to the country. Another though larger castle dominates
Bessonies, beyond St Hilaire — rather imposing in the sixteenth-
century style, with fine mouldings over each window and a
handsome portal in the east tower. The courtyard is now a
paddock grazed by *vaches de Salers* which stared at my approach

and snorted huffily like matrons disturbed at their household
occasions.

However, undoubtedly the handsomest and most complete
castle of this little region is that of Veyrières, at the charmingly
named Sansac-de-Marmesse. Easily missed because it lies (below
the main Figeac road) entirely concealed behind a screen of
immensely tall trees, it is best viewed from the lane leading round
behind the village or — if you are energetic and inclined to
trespass — from the water meadows by the Célé. So secret and
tranquil is Veyrières it appears to have grown out of and back
into the landscape: a neat *tourelle* at each corner of the *donjon*,
lauze-tiled eaves frowning gently over half-timbers that reach
down to its delicate *machicoulis*; a later central part with tall stone
chimneys, branching out into the garden; such detail hardly
evokes the aristocratic, slumbering charm of Veyrières on a hot
day when even the rooks talk softly to each other and the
murmur of doves invites one to lie full length among the daisies
and contemplate . . . nothing at all. Jean-Baptiste de Peyronnenc
de St Chamant, its most distinguished owner — he played a
prominent role in the wars of the Catholic League against Henri
IV — has such a long name one almost falls asleep over that too.

More active pleasures such as yachting can be enjoyed on the
broad, islanded stretch of the great barrage of St Etienne-
Cantalès, engineered out of the waters of the Cère, a few
kilometres south of the N.120. Lacapelle-Viescamp would make
an admirable place to stay; or St Etienne itself where, from the
mound below the church, there is a grand view across the water
to the wooded promontory that reaches out from the northern
bank. This barrage is a fine illustration of how to avoid
destroying a landscape by engineering works. Below St Etienne
the river resumes its normal width so that at Laroquebrou the
casual visitor simply would not suspect the existence of such giant
works. The town itself is well worth half an hour, especially if
one climbs up to the old castle whose terrace hangs over the
hugger-mugger of weathered roofs. It was owned by the Montal
family, well-known in Quercy. One of them, Louis XIII's
governor in the Guyenne, was assassinated in Paris in 1631; and
such was the poverty around here that at his funeral, when the
moment came to give alms to the poor, seven people died in the
crush.

The English, too, were hereabouts. Or so it would seem; for at

Montvert, just up the hill, is a crumbling manor behind high iron gates, with the arms of lion and unicorn emblazoned over the main door. The church in this tiny village is excellently restored Romanesque. East of Montvert we are soon over the border into the Corrèze.

IX

CANTAL: WESTERN HEIGHTS AND UPPER DORDOGNE

The main road from Aurillac to Bort, through Mauriac, dips up and down instead of following a ridge as one might expect from a quick glance at the map. This is because the rift valleys, splaying down from the Puy Mary reach right across to the Corrèze border to another barrage-system (using the river Maronne) at Enchanet. North of Mauriac a more jumbled sequence of valleys, following the line of the deepest one — the Vallée de Falgoux — twists north-west to merge into the gorges of the upper Dordogne. Between these two systems a narrow plateau, crossed by the D.22 at its widest point between Salers and Anglards, slopes gently in the direction of Pleaux, losing about a thousand feet in the process. All this is very fertile country, grazing land for the most part but rich in orchards and market-gardens around the villages and small towns.

From Jussac, on the N.122, a road leads off to Marmanhac where there are two châteaux; the more interesting of them, La Voûlte, is a rather curious building which one has to stand on the wall opposite to see. The otherwise excellent little book on the Cantal châteaux does not mention it so I will not go into detail; but it is certainly a collector's piece, architecturally speaking, the most surprising elements being a pert little bell-tower over the main façade and what looks, to the English eye, suspiciously like a lych-gate on the right. Marmanhac itself has the unfortunate distinction of a polluted stream — the only one I found in the Cantal! Further along, the road forks. We shall swing left to climb the ridge and drop down again into the next valley, over the col de Bruel, to reach Tournemire.

Here the castle of Anjony makes a most interesting visit (it is not, by the way, the castle of Tournemire at which the robber-baron Aimérigot le Marché took refuge only to be 'sold' to the

King by its tenant, for this has long since disappeared together
with four others that once brooded over this pretty valley). A
Sieur d'Anjony built it in 1439 with the approval of Charles VII
and it has the rare distinction of having remained in the same
family ever since. A very simple building, it is basically a
rectangular *logis*, with huge towers at each corner, crowned by a
roof-top walk. The best view is from the D.60, at a bend where a
plaque commemorates the death of a local doctor killed in a
motor-accident while on call. The interior is fascinating: from
the low, vaulted rooms at ground-level one climbs the tower
staircase to a majestic hall; this adjoins the chapel whose walls are
covered with fifteenth-century frescoes in good condition. On
the second floor — reached by the same 'master'
staircase — there are some remarkable paintings in the *Salle des
Preux*; ostensibly serious studies of historical characters and
episodes of chivalry, they were clearly done by an artist with a
rich if bizarre sense of humour so I will not spoil the surprise by
describing them (but do not miss Alexander riding an elephant
and David playing the harp on horse-back). At a more serious
artistic level the guide, an informed and amiable young man, will
show you a beautiful Byzantine silver crucifix of the sixth
century — a rarity in such country castles as this. More typical,
but in great variety and excellently displayed, are the old
weapons and hunting-trophies: I recall a boar-skin rug, the
fearsome head still attached, and a large hare, gruesomely splayed
on the wall, that fixed me with a gap-toothed, timeless grin.

The people around here, locked in their remote valley, appear
to have passed the time in constant feuding; a prior of Anjony
interred in a neighbouring church was dug up the same night and
deposited at the entrance to his own. They found the corpse in
the morning; or what remained of it — the rest had been
devoured by wolves! This macabre incident was part of a long
series of bloody clashes with the lords of Tournemire castle
jealous of the newly-arrived family of Anjony, whose power and
influence stemmed directly from the court of Charles VIII. Less
macabre is the story of two neighbours, Messieurs Muret and
Tremoulet. Each morning, Muret — loud-hailer in hand and
leaning on the branch of a handy tree by the stream — would
come to the water's edge and bellow insults at Tremoulet, who
soon tired of this long-range tirade. So one night he came out
and sawed the tree almost through. Out came Muret next

morning and took up his usual stance only to tumble, loud-hailer and all, into the stream.

The winding main road — if you can find somewhere to park, for the traffic is heavy — provides several excellent if momentary views down into this valley. Just above St Cernin there is a tantalising glimpse of Anjony, tucked into its hillside above the stream.

Many years ago I came to St Cernin in a rather ancient car, travelling with a friend. At the top of the hill a spring broke, jamming the brake-rod. Gingerly we trickled down into the village. The *garagiste*, a burly man with the deceptively impassive air these people have, shook his head: "*Ah! ça*", he muttered. "*Ça c'est difficile.*" We looked suitably helpless. He called out his son and they frowned over the mess. Eventually: "We shall arrange it", he said. I had the feeling he saw the job as a challenge. There was one snag from my point of view; I had no money as we had been on the way to Mauriac to cash a cheque. This I explained. He gave me a short, hard look and grunted: "Never mind, one can pay by postal order". His son then scoured the country, found a Citroen spring that might fit, cut it to size, worked all afternoon on the job. I forget what his father charged me but it was a small sum. I do remember his kindness and that of the *patronne* of the cafe nearby who lent us deck-chairs to while away the time in her garden. Which is why I tell the story.

One hears from English travellers in France of rudeness and unwillingness to oblige: I can only say that I have always found the people in these parts in the true sense hospitable, always willing to help when the need arises. Nor is the Auvergnat — in spite of his reputation — avaricious towards the visitor. Very, very rarely have I been overcharged for services rendered.

St Cernin church, in a hollow off the main road, is famous for its choir-stalls, easily the best in the Auvergne. Probably late fifteenth- or early sixteenth-century work, and said to have been carved for the monastery at St Chamant by artists from Toulouse, they make a rewarding study as one turns up each misericord to find some fresh delight. The Romanesque sculptures on the corbel-ends of the apse are also very good. Completely Romanesque churches are rare in the Cantal because there was so much destruction during the Hundred Years War and, later, during the Wars of Religion.

Half-way to St Martin Valmeroux a turning to the right leads to the handsome village of St Chamant, prosperous-looking, with a big church and a huge castle down the lane that one can easily miss. The church is finely proportioned, of the fourteenth and fifteenth centuries, but unfortunately rather dark. A pity because the woodwork, of which there is a great deal, rivals that of St Cernin: the stalls have human faces for poppy-heads and there are some lovely misericords; one of them, gently but firmly amorous, shows a courting couple engaged in their play. Nothing remains of the priory which presumably commissioned these late medieval carvings of such high standard.

From the east the château, towering above the fields, looks like a great stone galleon in dry dock. Like Veyrières, it has grown over the centuries yet somehow kept its architectural cohesion, rather as some English Elizabethan houses do. The *donjon*, with the original deep *machicoulis*, has been clasped into the main building by a seventeenth-century addition, itself a sizable 'house', at the east-end. The *corps de logis*, by its great height and steeply-pitched lauze roof, lends grandeur to the ensemble so that the total effect is of a measured dignity, *campagnard* but in no way bucolic, civilised yet unpretentious, an effect heightened by the fine trees and the informal gardens to which, when I was there, children's toys and a swing lent further charm. The castle, which originally belonged to the Escorailles family from nearby Fontanges, passed to that of Balzac d'Entraygues: Robert de Balzac paid for the rich wood-carvings in the priory-church whose 'chapter' he founded. He was chamberlain to Louis XI and the King's seneschal in Gascony. A later owner, Robert de Lignerac, was chosen by Henri IV to escort his estranged wife, *La Reine Margot*, from Agen to Carlat. In the late eighteenth century this family fell upon hard times and St Chamant had to be sold, to pay off debts, to the Couderc — prominent in the affairs of Aurillac — who own it still.

A steep lane climbs above St Chamant affording just one captivating glimpse of the castle's majestic *toiture*. After St Rémy de Salers, with a church so tiny as to fit (almost) into someone's back-garden, it drops sharply to Fontanges. The Scorailles family originated here and Louis XIV's pretty but silly blonde mistress was made its duchess. The château, behind a high wall along the Salers road, looks grim and silent as if it were still mourning the early, sad demise of this lady; but the village has a pretty green, shaded by the noble trees that grow so tall in these well-watered valleys, and its riverside is a popular camping-place. From here one may take the winding road along the valley of the Aspre, climb the Col de Légal and so loop back over the Col de Bruel to rejoin the 'Route des Crètes'; a beautiful trip on a fine day with the Puy Violent, the Roc des Ombres and the Puy Mary in full view (grand walking, too, but only for the strong in wind and limb). However, to reach Salers one has to go the other way.

The river Maronne, which has its source on the slope of the Puy Violent, hurries to St Martin Valmeroux past the restored Château de Palmont. A quicker way to Salers leads — I was about to say 'straight' but it has two wicked hairpins — up the ridge that provides this little town with such magnificent views. Just below the first hairpin is a mysterious and undocumented castle with several blue-capped turrets, so closely packed into the hillside it can scarcely be seen from above. Its roofs are only a few feet from the road, which then climbs viciously to Salers. Not a route for the weak in nerve or brake, let me emphasise.

I have visisted Salers at various times over the years, in good weather and bad, and especially in poor weather it always reminds me of a Scots Lowland town. The stone, like that of Fontanges, is very dark, more black than brown for it seems to get darker with time. There is no *bourg* in the upper Cantal more of a piece and certainly none in the whole region more picturesque, partly on account of its great height (some 3,000 feet), partly because it is so compact and architecturally well-preserved. Oddly enough, the town-walls were only added in the late fourteenth century after the English and the *routiers* had made free with Salers, a rare example of the 'open' medieval town. Its high prosperity came in the late fifteenth and sixteenth centuries when, the rude nobility of the Haute-Auvergne subdued by the crown or diminished by their interminable brawls, the town became a *baillage* and, like Riom, the residence of lawyers who served the regional government; hence the fine bourgeois houses that make such a handsome ensemble of the Place des Armes by the church and the Grande Place in the western quarter and lend it the rather severe yet elegant air of say, Perth or the Lowland Scots wool towns. Towers, courtyards, emblazoned doorways, sudden views of the hills on the far side of the Maronne valley, make the place highly photogenic.

The life of Salers now centres on the lower town in and

around the Place des Armes, below which is the principal car-park. A happy arrangement since the open space confronts the only ugly building, a barrack-like school whose brutal façade ought to shame the ministry responsible. From the west end of the Place d'Armes opens the chief shopping-street not yet entirely given over to tourist bric-a-brac and handsomely 'stopped', as it climbs, by the Porte du Beffroi, which has both bells and clock. My favourite shop is the chemist's which has in its window a bell-jar of 'pickled' snakes immersed for ever in intricate, unamorous coils; for what reason I have never discovered although a long screed relates the various mythical properties awarded to snakes, including (discreetly) their sexual role. In the hairdresser's window opposite, a large marmalade cat sometime sleeps and I was half-convinced, until it opened an eye at me one day, that it too was the stuffed emblem of something or other. Through the archway of the Tour d'Horloge one reaches the Avenue de Barouze, terminating in a massive arched gateway and leading into the open *Promenade* and the little garden whose belvedere provides a superb view up the Maronne valley. A thousand feet below lies the grassy bowl where the Maronne and the Aspre converge, with Fontanges in the middle distance, a blur of houses and tall trees.

The medieval castle on the northern outskirts has dwindled into a grassy mound, while the pastiche château off the Anglards road is now an old people's home. There remains the church whose sober exterior (the main door, only, is Romanesque, the rest fifteenth-century) matches its surroundings. The interior is extremely interesting for its tapestries, the two good Spanish paintings whether or not they are by Ribera, a fine seventeenth-century lectern similar to that at St Cernin and, above all, for the late fifteenth-century 'Entombment of Christ' in the Burgundian style; the three Marys and the apostles James and John mourn over the body of Christ, and two elaborately dressed figures at either end of the body presumably represent Peter and Matthew. The figures, sensitively grouped, are almost life-size, painted, and highly expressive in their grief. Such tableaux are quite common in Burgundy and we have noticed a less elegant example at Courpierre on the Dore; but the only one in the Auvergne to compare with this is at Montel-de-Gelat, which we shall visit as we go north into Combrailles.

In the nineteenth century, Salers became well-known for its cattle, thanks to a local agriculturalist, Tyssandier d'Escous, whose bust overlooks the Grande Place: it was he who revived and developed by selective breeding the long-legged purple-chestnut cattle now the principal wealth of this whole region north of the Aurillac. In such deeply-folded hill-country where the fields are necessarily small, farms are not large; yet a tenant-farmer with between twenty and thirty cows, fattening his beasts for market, selling his milk and breeding carefully, makes a good living. Usually, he owns his own house so he has few overheads, and his wife may cure her own ham and make and sell her own cheese. By British standards, the Cantalien farmer is by no means rich, although he lives well and appears content to follow his established way of life based on the traditional market fairs and church festivals. He has adapted slowly to modern scientific methods but since the war government services have done much to persuade him into the twentieth century and he now prospers, sending his children to good local colleges where they learn their farming or are encouraged to become mechanical engineers in the repair and maintenance trades. Except in Aurillac and Bort factories are few so, inevitably, many of the young people have to find a living elsewhere. However, building, or the conversion of old properties, provides a new and profitable occupation while the girls often find jobs connected with tourism, in the rapidly developing social services, or in the banks and service-trades.

It would be a pity to leave such a 'salty' place as Salers without one story, in this instance somewhat haunting, and reminiscent of the famous 'Appointment-with-Death-at-Samarra' folk-tale. It appears a certain André Pujom, in some minor legal difficulty, received a summons to present himself at the court in Riom-ès-Montagnes, to make his plea there. At the inn at Salers, over a round or two of drinks (the people here had a reputation for conviviality of a rather exuberant kind) some wag made an anagram on his name — *Pendu à Riom*. To this André took exception and a brawl ensued in which he was unlucky enough to stab a man to death. So he was brought to Riom the following day, tried and duly hanged. This tale — come to think of it — has a slightly sour Scots-Border tang, too!

From Salers there are two ways to go down into the Vallée de

Falgoux, perhaps the most beautiful of all the valleys in the Cantal: the more spectacular road follows the ridge as far as Néronne (little more than a hotel and a farm), then drops very sharply indeed through the woods along the *Cirque*, to the village of Falgoux itself. For sheer splendour of prospect this road rivals the 'Route des Crètes', especially on a clear, late afternoon when the declining sun throws the Puy Mary and the lesser peaks into sharp relief against a light-blue sky streaked with high cirrus cloud. The drop to the east is precipitous and there are several natural belvederes from which one may admire the views down into the Maronne valley or back west, as far as the eye can reach, to the wooded ridges above the Barrages d'Enchanet. Or there is a pleasant switch-back road across the narrow plateau to Anglards, a charming village now developing into a holiday-centre. It has one of the best bakeries I found in this part of the world, a turretted *manoir* and a little museum containing excellent tapestries. Its rebuilt Romanesque church, under whose apse-corbels bees nest every year, has an unhappy history: in 1422, when the great families of de La Tour and Tremoille were quarrelling over the inheritance of Jean de Bourbon, taken prisoner at Agincourt, the bravoes hired by Tremoille set the building on fire and massacred the villagers who had taken shelter there as they came out. Not content with this, they hanged two priests on trees in the little square before retiring to Salers to plot more mischief.

From Anglards a narrow lane dips down through the chestnut and beech woods to meet the perpetually winding valley-road just across the bridge over the river Mars, whose cascading waters race noisily down from the Puy Mary. At a certain point the manor of Baliergues can be seen, perched on a bluff above its terraced garden; while in the valley itself there are three small châteaux, the prettiest of them, Malprade — one of the most delightful *plaisances* in the Cantal — so demurely, daintily aloof, in its meadow below the road that one scarcely dares to trespass upon it. Further along is Chanterelle, very different in style; a rectangular, slab-walled fortress now shorn of its towers but endowed with a steep lauze-tiled roof, it passed by marriage to the Escorailles in 1664 and that family kept it until 1918, after which the place simply fell into ruin — a casualty, no doubt, of the impoverishment of provincial France after the first 'Great

War'. Only in 1960 was it bought and restored by a German industrialist, for his family to spend the summer there. Massive and functional, it symbolises the harder winter aspect of this countryside.

At St Vincent the valley begins to funnel towards its amphitheatrical rock-wall immediately below the Puy Mary. The bluffs on the northern side quite overhang the road, while the gentler slopes of the sharply-pencilled ridge to the south (that followed by the high road from Salers) are so beautifully set with trees, stretching benignly down to their meadow-terraces used for grazing, that no landscape-architect could possibly improve upon the natural scheme. The village of St Vincent — unlike Falgoux, higher up, which is ugly — nicely punctuates the valley at its mid-point; the snuggling thick-walled houses take advantage of every niche, fold and hollow as far as the stream which, everywhere else, can be heard rather than seen as it ripples coyly through tangle after tangle of thickets. Somehow this close-set huddle manages to contain both a castle and a church, the latter single-nave Romanesque with some rather lewd sculptures round the exterior of its apse. The château, which belongs to the de la Tour d'Etienne family, might have come out of Grimm's fairy-tales: it manages to be both sinister and cosy at the same time. On the western façade there is a gateway-arch, detached from the building itself and serving no practical purpose, with a blazon on one side and two warriors, sparring furiously, on the other.

It is said of the Cantal: "*Les vents se battent, les vents se contrarient, le temps se débat*". The weather can in fact change with singular rapidity. During the summer of '72, when I stayed one whole month at Le Vaulmier, I came to know that if the grey pate of Puy Mary was quite hidden by cloud rain was certainly on the way. On the other hand, so finicky are the winds playing the cloud above this valley-funnel that at seven o'clock one evening, as I returned home, the peaks along the Pas de Peyrol were gradually obscured by rolling tumulus; by 8.30 the whole sky was overcast, a lurid greeny-yellow at first, changing to red-streaked purple that cast an auto-da-fé shadow over the trees on the ridge; yet by 10.30 there was no cloud at all, every star in the firmament shining crystal-clear in a pellucid sky.

Beyond Falgoux, the D.12 bends sharply to climb the 'Cirque'

and achieve — after a steep, winding haul during which the
driver, at least, should pay no attention to the gorgeous
views — the cross-roads at the foot of the Puy Mary. Another
equally taxing climb, to the left, takes one out of the valley along
the northern scarp: at the top, a belvedere where they were
knocking-up a *buvette* in 1973 offers a magnificent view, the tall
steeple of Le Vaulmier marking that village like a raised pencil.
The woods of Marilvoux, now a park belonging to the local
commune, make lovely walking or picnicking. They extend almost
to Trizac, busily occupied with tourists in mid-summer, whose
church has a fine sculptured-wood altar-piece. High-plateau
country to the right — mostly well above 3,000 feet — cannot
be crossed by car, so one must follow the main Riom-ès-
Montagnes road, dipping and twisting at right-angles to the
series of steeply-folded valleys opening out to Bort. This
rhombus shaped piece of country formed by the N.678, the
valley road through the Gorges de la Rhue, and the *route nationale*
from Mauriac to Bort, contains some very pretty villages indeed
and most of them have excellent hotels (at Antignac, Saignes,
Champs-sur-Tarentaine and Menet, for example). Or, if you
prefer a small, lively township with good shops, Riom has much
to offer besides its immaculate early Gothic church with
interesting primitive Romanesque carvings on the capitals and on
the corbel-ends round the apse.

This is country to amble through with no particular end in
view, discovering what one may. Do not miss Menet, a few
kilometres west of Riom, for it has a charming lake to picnic by,
some of the best houses in this part of the Cantal and a most
interesting church — again, beautifully kept. The west portal is
austerely handsome, with two mythical figures, bizarrely carved,
helping to support it. The interior, finely proportioned, has
massive double-arches over the nave, good capitals, a seven-
windowed apsidal chapel and a handsome dome constructed on
an eight-fold hemispherical plan most unusual in this region (the
church at Lanobre is very similar, however).

From Menet a hatchwork of lanes cuts south-west to Auzers,
very high and with a grand view east towards the peak of la
Chassagne. The castle, whose gardens are cleverly devised to
make the best of this view, is quite delicious: fawn-coloured
walls picked out with dark-brown stone, deep *machicoulis*

terminating in dainty *tourelles* at each corner, a massive round tower on the garden-site, the western façade punctuated by a slimmer tower with three windows in line over the main portal, which has a Gothic arch and an escutcheon over the door. Of the original fourteenth-century building little remains for it was taken and burnt during the Hundred Years' War; what we see is an early sixteenth-century reconstruction virtually intact. This no doubt accounts for the sense of completeness it affords — neither medieval nor Renaissance but something delightfully in-between. Genealogically, Auzers is connected with both Fontanges and St Chamant; but it was a union between the families of Bompard and of Douhet (said to be Scots) which created the line that has owned it since 1470; a happy continuity since it has probably ensured the architectural integrity of this castle. An eighteenth-century d'Auzers, formerly a Knight of the Grand Cross of Malta, entered the service of Napoleon and became in 1808 — of all things — Commissioner of Police in Piédmont. However, he did so well at the job that the King of Sardinia offered him even higher responsibilities. These he modestly declined only to ally himself further to the Italian national destiny by marrying a local lady and becoming the uncle of Cavour. I would find it hard to choose between Auzers and St Chamant if asked to name my favourite large castle in the Cantal.

Of the other big villages Saignes is the most interesting, Antignac perhaps the prettiest, though St Etienne de Chomeil runs it close. Saignes was evidently a place of some importance; its medieval fortress is little more than an echo on the grassy mound which overlooks the town but there are two more castles in the vicinity, one a quaint pastiche, all turrets and roofs at odd angles, guarded by a posse of angry dogs whose barking sent me scurrying from the gates. Saignes itself has a pleasant square and several old houses to remind one of its Renaissance past. The hotels are modern but not excessively so, and their cuisine is to be recommended. The church is also good but that of Vebret, nearby, even better — country Romanesque with a handsome doorway and, inside, a fine 'Crucifixion', probably Romanesque and comparable with the superb twelfth-century Christ of Auzon.

Yet if one admires Vebret for its quiet sobriety and placid setting (the women of the village find the tree in its forecourt a pleasant spot for shelling peas or writing letters) Ydes, not to be confused with l'Hôpital Ydes, on the main road, is a gem. Within the entrance porch, on either side, are biblical scenes in low relief — on the left the Annunciation, Mary and the Archangel neatly framed by each arcade and, on the right, Daniel in the lions' den being rescued by the prophet Habbakuk, plainly brought to Babylon in great haste by an angel who grasps him firmly by the hair, while the prophet hopefully offers one of the beasts a 'cob' of bread as if uncertain whether Jehovah has a knack of dissuading lions. Inside there is an exquisitely carved wooden-pulpit with the whole mythology of the Temptation and the Fall winding up the balustrade of its stair; the reclining Eve has something of the sly sensuality of her counterpart on a famous capital in the cathedral-museum at Autun, in Burgundy. The animal- and bird-carving in this church is remarkable for its succinct realism — notice the bat on a capital in the south-side of the nave. Outside, over the handsome south-door, is St George striking at the dragon while all round the apse delicately carved grotesques and human heads witness the sculptor's originality and sense of style.

A narrow lane from Ydes runs up to Bassignac; its church has a good Romanesque portal and the *clocher à peigne* — tooth-comb bell-tower — almost universal in these parts. Opposite, on a high conical hill, a crumbling tower I had often noticed from the main road proved to be all that remains of the considerable castle of Charlus, from which Louis de Bourbon once had to winkle out the English. Of a later baron — very bored, it seems, in his eyrie — a slightly scabrous story is told: when his tenants came to pay their dues he demanded, for his amusement, not only their money but three skips accompanied by three of those noises of the baser kind usually called 'social errors'.

The two market-towns that serve this country on the fringes of the Upper Dordogne could not be more different in style. Mauriac, although a well-known holiday centre with excellent hotels, has retained its period allure; the seat of a minor bishopric and of the local assizes, it also has a pig-market along the curving outer boulevard at which one may test one's knowledge of *patois cantalien* as the burly farmers chaffer over their squealing beasts. The Romanesque church is famous for its west portal, round whose arch less ephemeral creatures from the Zodiac have been carved by a capable sculptor. Time-rubbed lions crouch on either side of the steps. The tower, several times remodelled, is extremely well-proportioned, and the apse one of the best of its kind in the Haute-Auvergne. Inside, one realises the great height of the building compared with the low-set churches of the surrounding countryside; but it is best seen before midday for there is not much light. Indeed, it was only during one of the evening concerts for which the basilica provides such an elegant setting that I was able to make out the features of 'Our Lady of the Miracles', yet another Black Virgin. Her plump cheeks and *retroussé* nose give her the look of Queen Victoria robed for a state occasion. The arcaded town hall has recently been rebuilt in suitable style but the best secular building is the so-called 'Chappe d'Auteroches' — now the law-court — which has the massive durable air of an ex-general; a place content to serve any and every purpose. A charming garden at the rear is usually guarded by an alsatian with no great liking for strangers. Close by is the *lycée* that serves as boarding-school, in winter, for the children from outlying villages; its 'classical' gate is a disaster, like some piece of Roman masonry half-begun and best forgotten.

Some parts of Bort are also better ignored, especially that along the river by St Thomas. The town is divided down the middle by the Dordogne, running fast and shallow. The upper town curls up and down about the massive church; the lower is mainly shops and railway station but by no means unattractive along the riverside. Previously best known for Les Orgues, the curious, tubular-shaped formations of rock above the D.127, Bort is now much visited for the lakes created by a dam across the Dordogne. This barrage — augmented by the Rhue whose waters are carried into it by artificial pressure through an underground pipe — is the controlling system for the whole of the Dordogne. Frankly, its huge concrete wall gives me the creeps as I cannot help imagining what would happen to Bort if some exceptional strain caused it to give way; but the reservoir itself fits happily into the natural grandeur of the hills and is being put to good use for boating, swimming and motor-launch excusions. These engineering works and services have contributed largely to the town's growth and prosperity (less than half the population is reckoned to be native to the region).

The lake's pretty upper reaches are best seen from Monestier, Confolent Port-Dieu or Singles. But the most popular attraction is the Château de Val, barely preserved from the waters on a little promontory reached by a turning off the N.122. A handsome fifteenth-century building, it could not be more picturesquely set. Now the property of the local *Commune*, which uses it to house summer-exhibitions of tapestries or paintings, it was once held by Dieudonné d'Estaing, who saved the life of King Philippe-Auguste on the battlefield in Flanders and prospered greatly thereafter. In the nineteenth century it came into the hands of the chocolate-family, Suchard, and there are some rather haunting photographs of this period in one of the rooms, showing how pleasantly situated the castle was in its original ambiance high above the gorge. Now, as a habitation, it is 'dead', the resort of casual visitors attracted here by the innumerable post-card 'views' sold all over the Auvergne. Still, it has survived one of the greatest landscape upheavals in central France and looks proudly over the blue waters, silent witness to progress in the shape of 'le water-ski' and sailing dinghies, and to the power of electricity.

After this it is pleasant to lunch at Lanobre, off the N.122 just beyond the turning to the castle. Spare a few minutes for the church here for it has some of the best 'storied' capitals in the Haute-Auvergne. Leaving the Dordogne and its attendant streams for the moment, drive across the upland road eastwards to the Lac de Crégut, part of another, smaller barrage system and a very pretty, tranquil spot indeed. Here, one evening, I saw a hawk side-slip with instant virtuosity to the placid surface and come up with a sizeable fish in its claws. South of Crégut, a lovely road through the Forêt de Maubert brings you to the N.679 which follows the gorges of the Rhue most of the way to Bort. Then, via the 'link' to St Amandin, climb onto the high plateau where a narrow road across bare, rolling country takes you through Lugarde (whose ruined chateau, if you can spare the time to walk, offers a superb view) and on to where three roads meet, one leading south to the pretty village of Cheylade, another to Ségur-les-Villas, once a Roman settlement, and the third to the substantial ruin of Apchon, which can be seen from various points on the roads above the Rhue — so high and isolated is it on a pinnacle of dark basalt that even Merle would have been hard put to take it. This was the senior barony in this part of the Auvergne and its *seigneurs* were remarkable for their unruliness. Perhaps because they claimed descent from the Romans, they bowed the knee to no mere Valois king unless forced to do so.

A few kilometres south of Apchon, beyond the village of St Hippolyte, is la Font-Sainte with a chapel to the Virgin on a rise above the fields. Here, on the last Thursday in August, takes place the celebrated 'feast of the shepherds'. They come here to give thanks to the Virgin for watching over them during their long pastoral vigil in these windy parts. Traditionally, this was the climax of the shepherds' year, and it must have been a very welcome break for they used to spend the whole summer here, two or, at the most, three together with only a tiny thatched *buron* or cottage for shelter. Pierre Besson, in his autohiographical story, *Un Pâtre du Cantal*, gives a vivid and moving account of the rough life a nineteenth-century shepherd led on these upland farms. As a boy, he himself was romantically drawn to the life and he describes the summer he spent with his childhood shepherd-hero, learning how to pasture cattle so that they fed off fresh grass each day, how to guard them at night, and the deceptively simple method by which the cheeses were made; one mistake and the whole batch was ruined, which led to the shepherd being instantly sacked on his return to the home farm.

One tale related to Besson shows how close to personal disaster these people were in their daily work: It happened that a shepherd carelessly allowed one batch of cheeses to turn sour as they hung from the roof of his *buron*. Taking them down he saw with horror that they were too far 'gone' to ripen — he would have to throw them all away and hope to find some plausible excuse when his master counted the moulds, or *fourmes*, at the end of the summer pasture. So he took them secretly to the edge of a cliff, and threw them down to rot in the undergrowth. Later he was able to convince his master that it had been a poor season. However, during the long winter evenings, after supper when there was nothing to do but doze in the communal living-room of the farmhouse, it fell out that he dreamed the events of the past summer — and talked in his sleep. His master, less drowsy, picked up a few words of this dream and, putting two and two together, was suddenly able to account for his poor 'crop' of cheeses. The next morning he gave the shepherd his pay and sent him packing. Now at this time, in spite of steady emigration from the Cantal, such responsible jobs were rare; once a shepherd had betrayed his trust no farmer would employ him. Desperate, and racked by his guilty conscience, the poor man committed suicide by throwing himself into a ravine.

The story has the melodramatic ring of a folk-tale but it is probably true; the farmers of the region were ruthless, grasping men who had succeeded only by being as hard as the rough country they worked. They could afford no slipshod or dishonest labour. Now, the shepherd has alternative sources of employment if the life proves too hard; he no longer sleeps in his 'buron' all summer for the ubiquitous motor scooter takes him up and down at will and the shift-system relieves his long hours. Yet this remains viciously hard country in bad weather. Sudden electric storms have been known to kill a dozen cattle before they could be brought to shelter.

Beyond La Font-Sainte there are still no roads across this high plateau, rising gradually to the knot of peaks around the Puy Mary: but one can walk, if so minded, to the wooded gulley of the Marilhoux stream and to the pass known as Col d'Aulac, by which we climbed out of the Vallée de Falgoux.

This excursion from the lyrically beautiful country about the gorges of the Rhue, rich in waterfalls and trout-streams, and rapidly developing as a *lieu de séjour* for those who prefer simple holiday pleasures, leaves only the western fringe of the Cantal between the Bort-Aurillac road and the Dordogne gorges to explore. These gorges, of a solitary grandeur that even the wilder parts of the Scottish Highlands cannot match, are so thickly forested and so sheer-sided as to be impossible of access except at points where roads have been built to serve the barrage-works and bridges to cross them. For these reasons it would be dishonest to pretend that this is good walking-country — one needs a car, if only to move camp from time to time from one site to another. The finest riverside roads are the so-called *Route des Ajustants* just across the Corrèze border on the right bank, and the short stretch between the Barrage de l'Aigle — perhaps the most beautifully sited of the dam-systems — and Pont de Spontour.

Further south the Barrage d'Enchanet, which utilises the Maronne, is being used as a leisure-resort. St Illide, whose over-restored church has some finely carved choir-stalls, and St Christophe both have hotels; or there is Pleaux, the local market-town, with a busy, workaday atmosphere and several sturdy bourgeois houses in the Renaissance style along the narrow streets between the *grande place* and the broad square where the market is held. (What open country there is above these deeply-folded, thickly wooded valleys seems highly fertile, which no doubt accounts for the excellent *pâtisseries* and *charcuteries* in Pleaux).

A few kilometres over the border, Rilhac-Xaintrie is worth the trespass for its robust dark-stone fortified manor, long since converted to mundane purposes, and for the huge stone-barn adjoining its farmyard, a durable momument to the country-mason's art if ever I saw one. Here I was pursued down the lane from the château-farm by a tiny milk-cart, donkey-drawn, in which a laughing child tugged helplessly at the reins. For some reason the donkey thought I might have sugar or a carrot in my pocket, or so the man in charge of it assured me when he caught up. I remember him for his startingly blue eyes and fair skin — certainly a racial throwback to Norman or Anglo-Saxon invader.

Very well worth visiting for its site is Branzac, haughtily placed on a spur of rock above the steepest section of the Maronne gorge. Still a very substantial ruin, it was built in the fifteenth century to replace an older medieval fortress. From the handsome stone-work of its windows and doorways it must have been an elegant château and there were frescoes on its walls, probably commissioned by Claude de Pesteils, whose family sponsored those we saw in the castle near Vic. Since he married a princess of the renowned and wealthy Carracciolo family of Naples, Italian artists may have been responsible. Fragments of colour are still visible here and there. But I remember the place for its superb, lonely site frequented, now, only by birds and rabbits.

Further north, off the N.680 near Ally, on a bluff looking across to the village of Escorailles, is the delightful Château de la Vigne whose L-shaped façade shelters a pretty garden, *un peu à l'Anglaise* with its rambler roses and flowering shrubs. François I de Scorailles built this place at the beginning of the sixteenth century when his medieval castle (still traceable in the village) went out of fashion. He could hardly have chosen a more

beautiful situation overlooking the wooded valley, with Drugeac
in the middle distance and the peaks of the Puy Mary chain just
visible from the upper windows. La Vigne can be visited but the
interior is by no means as attractive as its façade and the sylvan
opulence of its setting. It is now the property of Madame du
Fayet de la Tour (a branch of this family owns the Grimm's
fairy-tale 'manor' at St Vincent in the Falgoux valley). The
village, too, is highly attractive — one of those I have marked
out for my retirement should I ever achieve the moneyed state.
The lane down to the valley, passing through Drignac, offers
several views of the castle before turning sharply left over the
stream, to climb up to Drugeac, yet another charming village. It
has a tiny turreted *manoir* so private as to be almost invisible, and
an excellent hotel on the main street.

Within easy distance of these places is the remarkable
Romanesque church of Brageac, all that remains of a priory with
an interesting history yet so little known that Michelin did not
even mention it in 1972. An extremely early monastic foundation
dating back to the eighth century, it was started by St Till, a
monk from Solignac who practised medicine. Hence, no doubt,
the busts of St Cosmas and St Damian, martyred doctor-saints of
the third century and twin patrons of medical science. These are
said to have been brought back from the Holy Land by a lord of
Rilhac-Xaintrie. The present church, which has been carefully
restored, must have been here when a Benedictine order of nuns
took over the priory in the thirteenth century, for it seems to be
early Romanesque, austerely elegant, with nave and side-aisles
and three apsidal chapels; the capitals, mostly capped with foliage
or animal decoration, are good, while the sharply incised little
figures round the exterior of the apse — shoulders drawn down
to heels or clasping each other like primeval creatures startled at
being brought to light — make a fascinating study in grotesque
imagery. (The unusual and curious scroll-decoration at the base
of each pillar in the nave may offer a clue as to the builders, for
there are similar pillars at Mauriac and Ally.)

To the right, built into the nearest house, are vestiges of the
priory; a carefully trimmed, grassy belvedere all round the
church adds the final touch to a site which is quaintly and
uniquely beautiful, an admirable setting for its medieval hospital
to which the poor might come to find skilled care and advice.

Of the churches west of Mauriac only that of Champagnac-les-Mines, at the foot of a wide square lined by pleasant stone houses, compares with Brageac. It has been excellently restored and there are some fascinating capitals; the best of them, most ingeniously carved to take advantage of the available space, portrays St Michael cornering a delightful dragon (notice, too, the angel with a sharply pointed nose clinging to the underpart of the first capital on the south side of the choir). There are, also, an excellent font and a finely carved cupboard whose centre panel shows Christ's baptism by St John — not a church to miss. Immediately opposite are the handsome iron gates of an eighteenth-century château, so trimly and precisely placed beyond its garden, with a double staircase leading up to the main-door, that it might have been built for a film-set. Solitary and shuttered when first I saw it in spring, it was gay and all a-chatter with children in August.

The road from Champagnac to Serandou, and down the escarpment above the Dordogne to Pont St Projet, makes a picturesque trip. Not far up the N.682 a turning to the right through la Forestie peters out near a farmhouse: leaving the car here, I struck across the fields along a briar hedge so thick with butterflies it was like walking through a cloud of drifting feathers; the Auvergne countryside is peculiarly rich in butterflies, including the yellow and black swallow-tail, the large tortoiseshell and several varieties of fritillary. Across another field, almost invisible behind a thick screen of trees, are the ruins of the château called Miremont, one of the key-fortresses along the upper Dordogne. From here Madeleine de St Nectaire, of the family that held the castle in that proud place, rode out with her knights to challenge the Catholic besiegers. A young widow, beautiful and virtuous, she had inspired the Protestant forces about here to a vigorous resistance, and one story relates that she killed the King's lieutenant with her own hand. In the end an army under Montal — reputedly the ablest taker of castles on the Catholic side — was too strong for her so she was forced to retire, undefeated, to Turenne in the Corrèze. Though *classé monument*, Miremont is so overgrown that the trees have literally taken possession of the *donjon*, and it is dangerous to clamber about the ruins. But from the outer wall there is a lovely view across the forested hills to the Corrèze: as I leaned upon it a male buzzard, speckled brown and grey-white and large as an eagle, took off from his perch in a niche immediately below me and glided away, to circle the fields.

This seems an admirable point at which to leave the high country: romantic legend, ruined castle, nesting hawk, symbolise and evoke its beauty. Almost, one could wish that Miremont should never be restored but lie there, crumbling through time, the haunt of butterflies and cicadas, until the trees quite swallow it into their green shade.

X

COMBRAILLES AND NORTH-WESTERN MARCHES

"Land of hermits, knights and fairies", wrote Henri Pourrat; ". . . Combrailles is what remains of that ancient Auvergne which existed before the volcanoes". It extends in a shallow sickle-shape from the high table-land between Pontaumur and Bourg-Lastic, where outcrops of silver-streaked silicious granite break the soil, to the northern *limagne* east of the Riom-Ebreuil road. The further south one goes the more wooded it becomes — ash, birch and the lesser conifers predominating rather than the beeches and chestnuts that so enhance the landscape of the Cantal. In spring and early summer it is even richer in wild flowers, in great variety, than the Bois Noirs beyond Thiers: certain flowers and mosses only grow here, in fact, because of the mineral content of the soil, which includes sparfluor and barite. The Puy de Préchonnet, east of Bourg-Lastic, is the only volcanic cone, possibly the last hiccup of the prehistoric upheaval which raised the Chaîne des Domes. The landscape is rolling and open, while the hills sweep gently down to their valleys — in marked contrast to the sudden precipitous drops that characterise the volcanic country of the Monts Dore, the gorge of the Avèze (which marks the southern border of Combrailles) and the upper Dordogne. Another geographical feature along the eastern marches are the Etangs, or lakes, wide, reedy and uneven-shaped, quite unlike the volcanic crater-lakes we visited in the central *massif*.

Compared with the Haute-Auvergne, castles and historic monuments are few and there are only two great châteaux — Chouvigny by the Sioule, at the edge of the Bourbonnais, which can be visited; and Pontgibaud, on the lower Sioule, which cannot. This chapter, therefore, will not be a long one. Yet let no-one for whom scenic grandeur is not an absolute necessity be discouraged from visiting Combrailles; all of it is pretty and the Sioule valley extremely so, while the small towns like Giat, Bourg-Lastic and Montel as well as the minor spas of St Gervais and Châteauneuf-les-Bains are interesting and civilised, with excellent tourist facilities.

Bourg-Lastic, strategically situated at the junction of the N.89 (the Tulle-Clermont road) and the N.687, has a remarkable Romanesque church; a fusion of the limousin and auvergnat styles, the octagonal basilica-plan extending the choir into a single rounded apse (the lateral chapels were added later when it became necessary to enlarge the church). Structurally, therefore, the church is scarcely auvergnat at all but the great south-portal — its most striking feature — resembles those of Blesle and Mailhat while the carvings above the 'striped' pillars on the exterior of the apse also echo primitive carvings in the early auvergnat style, especially the handsome interwoven and the woodshaving motifs found all over the region.

There were several important medieval castles in the vicinity but these have disappeared; the biggest, which belonged to the Le Loup family, was that of Préchonnet: it was sold as a *bien national* after the Revolution and completely demolished. A descendant of this family, a lady-in-waiting to La Reine Margot at Usson, subsequently took to the religious life, founding several Convents of the Visitation at Riom, Montferrand, Clermont and elsewhere. Less happily, in July 1944, as the result of an ambush by *maquisards* near the bridge over the Chavanon, twenty-three men of the town were seized by the Germans, taken to the camp at Lastic (now a French army base) and shot. There is a sober monument to them in a clearing nearby.

The richly-wooded country between Bourg Lastic and Pontaumur makes delightful walking and from the road between Cisternes and Bromont there are striking views of the volcanic cones, posted like robot sentinels on guard over some forbidden *enceinte*. Herment is a sleepy little place, amiably situated on its hill; the view from the esplanade by the war memorial is splendid and the church, part Gothic, part Romanesque, worth going into. The town is very up-and-down and the older quarter seems a trifle forlorn — the life has ebbed to the part along the main road where the hotels are, and one of these serves excellent food. Giat is a livelier place, perhaps more typical of the Creuse than the Auvergne; but then the people here, in what used to be called 'la Marche', are a mixture, too — no less reticent, but lighter of complexion and hair. The main square, its houses painted in all shades of fawn, beige and cream (the shutters picked out in green and red) is a diverting *mélange* of architectural styles that somehow compose into a most agreeable whole. The family of the wicked Baron Pierre, court-intriguer and wifekiller, whom we encountered at Châteaugay, originated here. The mound where their castle stood has been turned into a pretty public garden. Beyond Giat, up the D.13, is the slightly mournful Etang de Tyx, a wide stretch of placid greeny water that looks as if it would make good coarse fishing. But I suspect it belongs to the restored Château de Marcollanges on the right bank for its borders are marked private and there is a system of sluices leading to the lake from what look like fish-breeding ponds in its back garden.

At the junction of the D.13 and the main Aubusson road, St Avit might not seem to offer much. In fact it has a distinctly original Romanesque church. The little tower, crowned by a spirelet, at once strikes a note of eccentricity, while inside there are several fascinating capitals remarkable for their originality of treatment and for the way bright colours are used to enhance the detail of their design. There is one unusually luxuriant, flowing acanthus, a quaintly affecting Adam and Eve, a pair of eager-looking angels, one painted a gay sky-blue with a honey-gold nimbus, and two naked winged-figures, eyes agog, kneeling to clasp a shield between them. Combrailles is rich in surprises of this kind.

In the countryside hereabouts one notices, especially in bright sunshine after a shower of rain, the silvery-grey lichen that clings to stone-work, wooden fencing and bridges, and to the bark of trees. It is as if some mildly paranoiac scene-painter had been at work diligently creating a universal décor for *Sleeping Beauty*; everything glistens and sparkles, reflecting the clear swift water of the innumerable brooks and rivulets that feed the lakes. Montel, a few kilometres from Chancelade, the largest of these *étangs*, has another interesting church, much larger and more imposing than St Avit. The interior seems a trifle cold at first but it has the spacious elegance of many Limousin churches and it contains the only 'Entombment of Christ' to rival that of Salers: the women grouped behind the body of Christ are all of a family, with thin lips and pinched, aristocratic faces drawn with sorrow; while the figure on the right has remarkably haunting eyes as if he looked beyond the tomb to other agonies to come. There is also a good Pietà in the Flemish-Burgundian style and, in lighter vein, an unusually expressive St Roche (his wholly dog carries such an enormous stone in his mouth one wonders how ever he picked it up!).

Still further north lies Auzances on a hill above the Cher, at a crossing where five roads meet. Evidently a fortified town from its position and from the way the streets curl into the huddle of old houses around its central square. The big twelfth-century church — in bad shape, I was told by the old lady arranging flowers in the choir, until it was restored in 1966 — is covered with frescoes; not Romanesque or even late Gothic but modern 'Byzantine', by a Russian artist now living in the Pyrenees. They are extremely good paintings, freshly conceived and admirably adapted to the dimensions of the church, using the typically Byzantine technique of moulding the garments to throw the modelling of the figures into bold relief. The artist has used a limited range of colour, mostly restful blues and dark reds: those in the chancel, however, have been left in outline, the forms delineated by chalky red brushwork (to avoid overwhelming the church with too much colour, my informative lady remarked). Auzances, though busy and apparently prosperous, retains its period atmosphere. There are some handsome bourgeois villas along the hill leading out to the Evaux road and the townspeople are trying to attract visitors by staging a modest arts-festival each summer.

Striking east from Auzances along the narrow D.4A one comes first to Verghéas, situated in a hollow with the handsome stone farm-houses and massive barns characteristic of this fertile country. Its Romanesque church, burned down 200 years ago, is the object of a pilgrimage in honour of a 'miraculous' Virgin brought back from St Louis's crusade by three knights, one of them from nearby Roche d'Agoux, second of the three castles in Basse-Auvergne set up by Alphonse de Poitiers to control the western approaches to the Auvergne. The Lady of Verghéas has a long, plump-cheeked face with gentle eyes and a full affectionate mouth. More English or northern French than Eastern, although the statue is said to have been carved in Palestine, she sits, feet planted wide apart, in a stoutly made rustic chair. The Child, with alert gaze and right hand lifted in blessing, stands upright in her lap. The church has been rebuilt in simple, blunt Romanesque style and the stained glass windows in the apse and south chapel, dedicated to St Roche, are extremely good modern work in rich colours, the white of the garments used to highlight deep scarlet-red, blue, old gold and purple. A plaque on the north wall commemorates the 'crowning' of this Virgin by the Archbishop of Bourges, on the authority of Pope John XXIII. One feels the old man would have like this country shrine. On the floor is a stone slab fondly remembering the last *curé*, who guided this parish for forty-five years. The Virgin, gentle though she seems, was once angry enough to strike three drunken mockers deaf, blind and lame; but she also made a child crippled from birth walk; and, in the 'Great Fire', saved the house of a man with the presence of mind to seize the statue from the burning church and carry it in his arms round and round his cottage in simple trust that she would reward his faith.

Roche d'Agoux, a great fortress in St Louis's time — its dominant situation commanding the March explains why — is no more than a jumble of stone on a mound. A more interesting ruin, though it is sad it should be so, is the former abbey of Bellaigue, above Pionsat. This must have been a rich Cistercian abbey, built in the twelfth and thirteenth centuries, and it contained the tombs of Archambaut III de Bourbon and his wife Beatrix. Left to moulder during the past 200 years the church has recently been given the protection of a wooden roof, and there were signs, in 1972, that the Beaux-Arts were beginning to take an interest. They certainly should, for it is a great shame such a substantial ruin be left to crumble. At the moment it serves as cow-shed to the adjoining farm in whose paddock — perhaps the cloister — a marble cherub reigns forlornly over wasted eminence.

Both Pionsat and Montaigut-en-Combrailles, on the Montluçon road, are pleasant small towns; the former has a main-square of noble proportions, a handsome but coldly restored church and a north gate which once formed part of the château built in the time of Henri IV — one of those aristocratic houses that has merged into later domestic buildings to form a pleasantly inconsequent ensemble, with gardens reaching down to the little river Boron. There is nothing industrial about Pionsat but Montaigut, a steeply twisting place with a ruined castle and another fine church — basically Romanesque — that has only recently been restored, now almost joins St Eloy-les-Mines: this town, like Brassac and St Florine below Issoire, thrived on coal-mining in the late nineteenth century and the first two decades of our own (which no doubt accounts for the presence here of blonde, blue-eyed people, Poles who emigrated to St Eloy to find work before and after the First 'Great War'). Brassac has succeeded in attracting new light industries but St Eloy is still seeking fresh outlets, for the mines have for some time been uneconomic.

Part of the labour-force has gone to the hydro-electric system — the largest in central Auvergne — developed from the swiftly running waters of the Sioule, extending from Les Ancises (an ugly village that does no credit to the regional authorities) to Queuille. The gorges are very steep here and the country unusually wild and remote for Combrailles. There are, however, several beauty spots easily accessible by car, notably the waterfalls at Montfermy, off the very pretty corniche road from Pontgibaud to St Gervais; and, beneath a thickly wooded bluff which drops sheer to the Sioule, the overgrown ruins of the Chartreuse de Port St Marie, a favourite resort of fishermen after the trout for which this river is so noted. Also, if you like a singularly handsome piece of man-made grandeur to go with your scenery, the artificial lakes beneath the towering steel tracery of the Viaduc des Fades, reputedly the highest railway-viaduct in Europe. The plateau to the east of the Sioule levels out at some 2,500 feet, rising steadily towards Manzat until, near the hamlet of Sauterre (with the volcanic cone of the Puy de la Louchardière looming up to the south) it achieves 3,000 feet and a very fine view. Another grand prospect can be found at Comps, down a narrow lane off the D.62, worth visiting, too, for the early Romanesque church which has good 'interlaced' capital decoration and, inside, a curiously moving rustic Pietà; the blue robed Virgin is primitive, almost pathetic in the sculptor's attempt to convey emotion, the Christ a man-child clasped into her lap by strong, prehensile fingers.

Above the 'barrages', the Sioule finds an easier path to the dainty little spa of Châteauneuf-les-Bains, a watering place in miniature, most prettily set beside the stream, the newer part very spick and span with a good modern hotel and some solid summer residences. Up the hill and several minutes' delightful walk from the bridge across the Sioule, the blue-tiled roofs of a Second-Empire château peep through the trees into whose luxuriant green a tiny church seems to nestle for shelter. When I was there in June, a young man was busy restoring one of the nearby cottages while an older resident and his wife have converted another into an art-gallery. The church itself, immaculately kept, shows much evidence of tender care for it has been restored in excellent taste: a trunk of beech-wood has been cleverly cut to serve as an alms-box while the altar, totally effective in its rugged simplicity, has been fashioned out of a single three-ton block of Volvic stone. One massive round arch separates nave from choir and two fine wooden figures of St Cyr and St Valentine (the patron saint) decorate the apse. All this restoration has been done at the parishioners' expense over the past few years, a striking example of the Auvergnat's undemonstrative pride in his religious tradition and his ingenuity in using local materials to embellish it. The esplanade behind the church offers a lovely view over the several hamlets of the spa — a *mélange* of blue and pinky-russet roofs and white and fawn walls, the thickly wooded bluff reaching down to them and closing the valley at one end so that the whole place seems private, immune from the hurrying world in a wholly natural way. One can imagine no more sympathetic ambiance in which to ease the nervous ailments the waters of its volcanic springs are said to cure.

Down-river again, beyond Lisseuil, the Sioule (hitherto so thickly bordered with trees as to be almost invisible at times) suddenly carves out for itself a tiny plain. The force of the current has thrown out alluvial soil on the 'open', weaker side of its course, while the bank on the western side, though under-cut, has remained higher. Here the main road forks to climb up to St Rémy-de-Blot, and through the village a narrow lane winds to the imposing ruin of Château-Rocher, built on the model of Rochard Coeur de Lion's Castle Gaillard, on the Seine. If the weather has been wet, as it was when I came here in May, be well advised and leave your car in the village; for mine became firmly stuck in the mud sluiced out of the high banks on either side by a heavy shower and was only persuaded on and up by a group of kindly students who happened to be on a working trip to St Rémy, helping to restore the castle. Château Rocher — so superbly placed above the Sioule as to rival the solitary grandeur of the Château d'Alleuze on the Truyere — was erected by a Bourbon in the thirteenth century. Pourrat, who rarely misses such an opportunity, relates of its huge kitchens, still there to see, that they were the haunt of witches in the habit ". . . of roasting for the 'sabbath' a tiger spitted with cartwheel nails". Surely one of the strangest origins recorded of the 'cuisine auvergnate'? Evidently witches of formidable digestion whom the spirit of St Rémy, hovering nearby, would have had some trouble in exorcising.

A couple of kilometres further on, the Clermont-Montluçon 'route nationale' does not, now, cross the Sioule by the fine humped-back Pont de Menat, at least 200 years old and notorious as the scene of dreadful accidents in stage-coach times. Presumably the steep descents either side were too great a hazard for iron-shod hoofs in icy weather. The village of Menat, just off the main road towards Montluçon, repays the detour for it has a huge Romanesque church and a chapter-house, all that remains of the famous seventh-century Benedictine abbey. The fine ogival west door is certianly transitional but the interior contains a wealth of twelfth-century sculpture. Splendidly luxuriant foliage capitals abound, while in the south aisle occurs, in peculiarly vivid form, that strange marriage of beast and man so favoured by the darker side of the medieval imagination, the two human heads peering out in dumb astonishment over smooth, primeval bodies; and in the chancel is a superbly malicious serpent capable of seducing any Eve yet born. This church, built on treacherous foundations, almost collapsed in the fourteenth century; which accounts for the *charpente* roof — replacing the Romanesque vault — and the mutilated east end without ambulatory and chapels, lost in a further nineteenth-century restoration. Even so, as Craplet remarks, Menat must have been a highly original building, scarcely resembling in structure or in certain details of its carving the great churches of the auvergnat 'Limagne'. The cloister, in a sad state of disrepair, was being put to rights in 1972 and one can only hope for an eventual restoration as careful as that at Lavaudieu. The village, as usual in Combrailles, has some fine solid houses that will surely resist every ravage of time and weather.

East of the main road the Bourbonnais border dips sharply south to follow, for several miles, the winds of the Gorges de Chouvigny. St Gal is another pleasant village with a lovely old mill by the riverside; but the focal point of a trip along this gorge must be the castle of Chouvigny — with Cordes the most remarkable example of cultured restoration in the Basse-Auvergne.

There is no village along this gorge until one reaches St Gal. The crossing at Chouvigny below the castle was strategic, established by the Romans who called the place Calvinacium. Until 1903 it was the only place at which to cross the river and medieval pilgrims, passing from the abbey at Ebreuil, downstream, to that of Menat, on their way to Compostella, no doubt used the path the Romans cut along the rock-face to reach the ford. They could then be escorted through the forest along the left-bank by horsemen from the castle. Otherwise, the Sioule — then navigable — was the easier and safer route.

The family of de Chouvigny (or Chauvigny) was well known in the Bourbonnais in the eleventh century; Guillaume is thought to have built the castle around 1250 and his descendants kept it until it passed, by marriage, to the de Montmorin in the middle of the fifteenth century. Pierre de Montmorin and his son, Jean, were both knighted by Charles VII on the field of Bayonne, while a descendent, Annet, governed the Bourbonnais until 1555. With him the male line ended and the inheritance passed to the Motier de La Fayette, with whom it remained until 1734. This branch of the La Fayette were quite a distinguished lot and they married well (into the Bourbon-Busset, whose great castle still adorns that village on an escarpment above the Allier, near Vichy, and into the dukedome of Tremoille). The most interesting personalities are Louise, lady-in-waiting to Anne of Austria, who was courted by Louis XIII but resisted his advances and died a nun in 1665, and Madeleine, who wrote — as we noted at Chavaniac — about marital virtue in *La Princesse de Clèves*. Perhaps because of the former La Fayette connection the castle was seemingly unmolested during the Revolution and remained intact until sold to the Duc de Morny, described by a modern historian as "perhaps the most brilliant, unscrupulous, and from a

political point of view, the ablest and wisest" of Louis-
Napoleon's ministers. Despite — or perhaps because of — his
singularly 'mixed' ancestry (he was the son of Hortense
Beauharnais, Louis Napoleon's mother, by her lover, de Flahaut,
himself an illegitimate son of Talleyrand) Morny was an unusual
combination of the dashing and the shrewd: he favoured the
steady evolution of parliamentary government in France, and his
early death in 1865 left the Emperor without a strong liberal
adviser in the years of crisis, 1870 and 1871.

The castle's distinguished past ownership is fittingly reflected
in its present immaculate state of preservation. The Duc de
Morny lopped the east tower by thirty feet or so, for reasons of
safety, but his other and less happy adjustments have been put
right by the present owners, so that the buildings stand, now,
virtually as they were in the fifteenth century when de
Montmorin acquired the castle. At the north corner-end is a stout
watch-tower on whose battlements lanterns were lit to
communicate with the Château-Rocher, up-valley. A square
donjon overlooks the gorge, while there are two other towers, the
eastern one formerly a prison, remarkably intact curtain-walls
and a charming terrace-garden which has, presumably, replaced
the medieval exercise-yard.

The interior matches the exterior for elegantly functional
simplicity and one may admire the cunning arrangement of the
defences in the *tour de guet* (or watch-tower) which enabled
archers to pour a withering fire on sappers attempting to mine
the walls without putting themselves at risk. In the ogival-
vaulted oratory is a rare example of the Virgin portrayed with
breast exposed — rare because a fifteenth-century Pope forbade
the making of such statues though he neglected to order the ones
already carved to be destroyed. A chimney in such a room would
seem unnecessary; in fact, it disguises the entrance to a passage
leading down to the river. For the rest, there is some unusually
fine armour, a remarkable Swiss-clock whose pendulum
movement is too violent for it to be used, and a beautiful chest
from India whose decoration records the landing of French
soldiers at Pondicherry and what they saw on arrival.

Almost, one feels, Chouvigny is too beautifully precise in its
restoration, so nicely and formally is everything placed. But it
can hardly fail to interest even the most unhistorically minded of

visitors; and it makes an interesting contrast with Davayat, the little *Louis-Treize* manor a few miles down the road to Riom, all cosy domesticity and intriguing bric-a-brac.

That the church at St Hilaire-la-Croix should not be mentioned in the *Guide Vert* seems strange; for it is still a fascinating building, set proudly on a green and quite unencumbered by houses. The north portal is perhaps the finest in Combrailles, multi-arched with exquisite interlaced capital-cushions and some fine grotesques; the outer arch-moulding must once have been entirely covered by carvings of the saints — a few remain — and the inner arch is cusped, so the doorway is probably late twelfth century. Inside, two lovely capitals are used as fonts and on the west wall stands a rather bitchy-looking Virgin whose sly down-curving mouth reminded me of the Judith in the great basilica at Albi, on the Tarn. One notices, too, the same coyly-skirted St Michael, pinning his bearded devil, as at Loubeyrat, further west on the Châtel-Guyon road. But the most memorable sculptures are the two fork-bearded heads, one above the other, on the corbel-ends of the chancel arch; the uppermost appears to lean through his own thighs while, right and left, are two smaller heads — one demonic, mouth agape, the other youthful and mournfully human. Another pillar has unusually well-preserved renderings of familiar Auvergnat themes: the usurer being led away by devils and above it, as if to refute the inevitability of such damnation, the two hook-beaked birds sipping eternal life from the chalice.

Yet, having described all this to entice the passing traveller from an unusually fast section of the N.143, I can only guess that *Guide Vert* was ashamed, for this church, a particularly fine example of late Romanesque, was in 1972 in a disgraceful state, green with mould in the chancel, the plaster ceilings peeling and unkempt. Birds fly in and out of the west window to further soil the cornices while an ugly and secular window has been let into the wall behind the stoop. The village, too, has a neglected air; several houses on the main street are shuttered and silent, mere facades behind which weeds and shrubs rampage in anarchy. In curious contrast — when I was last at St Hilaire — well to-do young people, Minis and Peugeots parked behind the apse, were playing football on the green while their barbecue smoked and a spitted lamb awaited its final, culinary moment. Then, as I turned to leave, I saw right in the middle of the wide village pond a statue of Christ, sternly pointing. I wondered whoever put him there and why. At any rate, in the context of a dilapidated church and the disregarding laity "caught in their sensual music", the statue seemed weirdly symbolic, awash in its reedy pool.

The restored and tidy church in Volvic stone at Loubeyrat is a better note on which to end. And — a final grace-note of natural beauty — between here and Charbonnier-les-Vieilles is the most attractive lake outside the mountain-country, the Gour de Taxenat. It is so nearly round and so near the '*Chaîne de Volcans*' it must be a crater. Let Henri Pourrat, who is very fond of this corner of the Auvergne, describe it: "a disc-shaped lake two and a half kilometres round, mirror of greeny gold richly edged with silver, which from the surface of its waters reflects the zenith and lays beneath us the clear gulf of the heavens". Taxenat, whose northern slopes are bright with broom in early summer, has the quality of trance-like stillness so often encountered in the Auvergne that one does not exaggerate in calling it 'haunted'. Yet here this quality is gentle, acceptant; quite unlike the sinister cobalt depths of Pavin, in the Monts Dore, which Wagner might have imagined. The two lakes may symbolise the two natures of this country.

The shores of Taxenat are private: but, as one often finds in the Auvergne, no-one seems to mind if you stroll about them.

Quite near here is the hamlet of Rochegoude where the uncle of the Napoleonic general, Desaix, used to plant an oak tree at the birth of each nephew. It is said the one planted for this hero ceased to grow the day he was killed at Marengo. Which brings us back to Clermont, where his statue on the Place de Jaude faces that of Vercingétorix: another fruitful conjunction of opposites in the nature of this region.

ENVOI

I only hope the Auvergne will somehow retain its secret, haunted quality. Certainly, now that Monsieur Giscard d'Estaing, the mayor of Chamalières, has become the President of France, the people can be trusted to make the most of this honourable family connection. There is nothing wrong in ambition used to good ends; and the Auvergnat has earned his prosperity, as I trust I have made plain.

The geographer, Lucien Gachon, reminds us that the silences of this countryside are reflected in what he aptly calls "l'air caché" of the small houses along the banks of the furiously hastening Couze and other small rivers, adding that there are many other villages still more hidden from the light of day — the caves in the escarpments which contain cheeses, wine, and fruit stored to ripen.

These are truly private places, roadways barred from the outside world by great oaken doors. From time to time, in one of these 'dédales de terre', a passage gives way underfoot to reveal a deep hole, perhaps to revive in the mind of the country-people the legend that the 'great' always founds a means of escape in time of war. A castle was taken, pillaged, its men-at-arms strung-up, massacred or thrown from the walls; but the young châtelaine herself found a way out, deep into the surrounding woods, to meet some cavalier who made her princess of a new castle encircled, this time, by a moat whose waters young peasants would thrash by night, so that the croaking of frogs should not disturb her sleep.

Romantic legend? or — perhaps — an unusual variation of the marian cults which so pervade the Auvergne. In such a country, stories of this kind well up into the consciousness of a people that acknowledges, without altogether accepting as ultimate 'truth', the mundane realities of our scientific world.

The Auvergnat has, of course, long since abandoned such medieval attitudes just as the nobility open their castles to visitors or as *colonies de vacances* for city children: they live, for the most part, off their investments in Paris, returning only for the short, hot summers so liable to be interrupted by cataclysmic storms. When these occur the traveller may recall that the whole area was born of a geological cataclysm, that huge rending of basic matter which threw up the majestic chain of volcanic peaks. Scarred, eroded, constantly changing with the passing of season and weather yet always the same in the brief time-scale of human existence, their haunting — and haunted — presence dominates the mind long after one has left the Auvergne.

BIBLIOGRAPHY

There is virtually nothing in English on the Auvergne as a whole. For the casual visitor who can read French, I recommend the excellent series published in Clermont by Editions G. de Bussac: *Châteaux Vivants d'Auvergne* and *Châteaux Vivants de Haute-Auvergne*; and on the churches, *Eglises Romanes en Auvergne* with text by Bernard Craplet. Other useful pocket-books are *Châteaux du Cantal* by Bouyssou and Muzac and *Châteaux de la Haute-Loire* by the Duc de Polignac (Nouvelles Editions Latines). Bussac also has a series of booklets on towns and districts of particular interest, many of which are now being revised and reprinted — but only in French.

The most entertaining book on the region, and one to which I am greatly indebted, is *En Auvergne* by Henri Pourrat (Arthaud). Lucien Gachon's *L'Auvergne et Le Velay* is excellent on the geography and the social background. The best short history is by Rigodon in the *'Que Sais-je?'* series (Presses Universitaires), while a very readable and concise one is by A.L. Manry, who teaches history at the Lycée Pascal in Clermont. Pierre Estienne, *Villes du Massif Central*, is good on the economic background, while Ronserail, in *L'Auvergne: Autrefois, Aujourd'hui*, tells some amusing stories about nineteenth-century Clermont. Finally — very elegant and expensive but with a good text — there is *Merveilles des Châteaux d'Auvergne et du Limousin*, edited by Conchon.

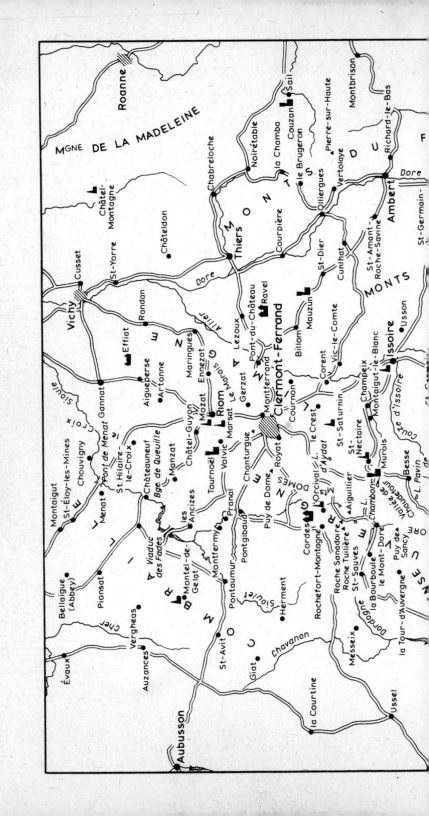

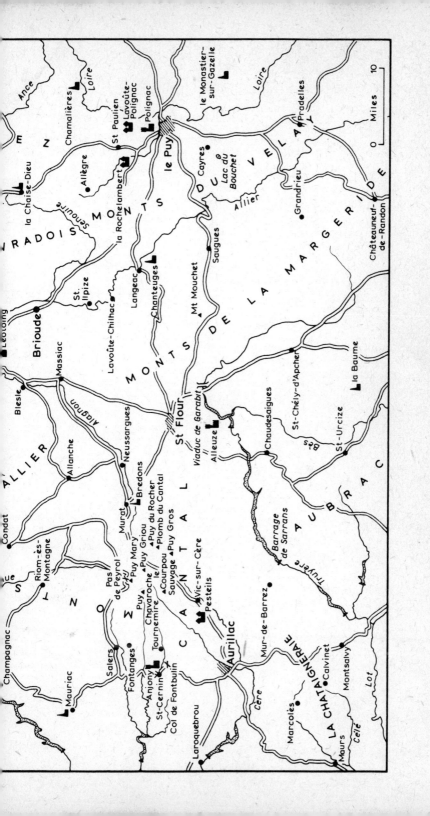

INDEX

INDEX